THE BULLET IN MARY'S CROWN

The Story of Our Lady of Fatima

Mr. F. Robert Roche, O.P., A.B.

Visit our website at www.StillwaterPress.com for more information.

First Stillwater River Publications Edition

ISBN-10: 1-946-30038-1
ISBN-13: 978-1-946-30038-6

1 2 3 4 5 6 7 8 9 10
Written by F. Robert Roche, O.P., A.B.
Cover Design by Mikahla Dawson
Published by Stillwater River Publications, Glocester, RI, USA.

DEDICATION

I dedicate this book to the memory of

Mark C. Dean

who learned high school chemistry from me as a teenager, made me proud upon graduation from Harvard "Magna Cum Laude" and who helped proof read this text for me upon his retirement as a scientist. Few have ever had a more devoted, shy, and thoughtful friend. He is greatly missed by all who knew him.

Table of Contents

Map of Portugal

PROLOGUE

Many books have already been written about a series of events which took place nearly a century ago. They tell of that splendid Lady chosen by God to give a human body in which His divine person could visit the world, redeem His people, and open wide the gate of heaven to humanity. Her visit to Fátima in Portugal was not unique; for She has made many visits to earth from Her throne in heaven over the past twenty centuries.

Each of Her visits has had a specific purpose. Yet Her visit to Fátima was different in that She had a most unusual task of saving the life of Her devoted servant, Pope John-Paul II, from an assassin's bullet without ever breaking Jewish law which forbids "fortune telling". Only mystical prophesy as in ancient times could be used. And so She began early in the century when Europe was at War and the evil of Communism was spreading from country to country to draw mankind back to sanity.

Her visit was to make a profound impression on mankind for prayer while the mystery of Her visit unfolded during the course of the century. As decades passed, books were written by those who witnessed the events. This book will draw on some of this previously collected and verified data, as well as some of this writer's personal research and experiences during several visits to the sites of the holy phenomena.

From my former summer home on the Portuguese island of Terçeira in the archipelago Açores, it is only a two-hour flight to the Lisbon airport and an hour drive north to Fátima. There, a bustling

1

town of several hospitals, numerous hotels, and several convents of religious orders surround the magnificent Basilica Shrine to the Virgin Mary where thousands of pilgrims arrive daily to pray, make reparation, and attend daily Masses celebrated by priests from many lands and tongues. A great wealth of information and inspiration can be brought back from this wonderful place honoring the Virgin Mary, a place where in 1917 lay only a remote pasture for grazing sheep.

As a Dominican lay brother, the Virgin Mary has been my patron saint and guide in my journey to paradise. This is true for many who realize that John, a courageous teen, the only male at the foot of the cross and therefore was "head" of the new tribe of Christianity, received Mary for us as our mother from Christ Himself with the words, "Mother, behold Thy son (John), and son, behold they Mother". And thus, She became the Blessed Mother of all Christians for all time. As is true of mothers, Mary has kept Her eyes on us, Her children, throughout history. Appendix B lists many of Her documented visits for guiding Her people.

To ensure that he could look after Mary throughout her life, John was given a mantle of protection from enemies allowing him to live nearly a century, unlike the other apostles who were soon martyred. His gospel, written late in life, is deeply retrospective.

In addition to the chapters which tell the story of what happened at Fátima, a great deal of information is included at the end of this book to assist those scholars seeking additional information. Appendix A lists all the bishops of the former Lèiria Diocese and the current Lèiria-Fàtima Diocese. Appendix C lists the Popes of the Twentieth Century of which a number were deeply involved with the Fátima events. Appendix D gives the chronology of the Fátima events. And Appendix E lists several books written during the past century which provided valuable information from many first-hand witnesses of the events of 1917 as well as a list of the scholars who proof read our manuscript and made suggestions for its improvement.

The Bullet in Mary's Crown

One of these scholars, Mark Dean, who was a chemistry student of mine in the early 1960's, passed away in February 2016 of kidney failure at age 73. After his graduation from Harvard (Magna Cum Laude) and service in the U. S. Air Force (with honors), he furthered his education in California remaining there as an industrial chemist until ill health forced his early retirement at age 62. Although a non-believer, his careful scientific objectivity kept accuracy in this text. And so this work is dedicated to his memory.

Appendix F is the Index and other acknowledgements; and Appendix G gives the full text of Rev. Manuel Ferreira's letter to the editors of the Lisbon and Oùrem newspapers.

We begin with the narrative of Mary's greatest visit to earth early in the twentieth century: a turbulent time with many great wars, the attempted annihilation of Judah, the attempt of a papal assassination, and the threat of nuclear annihilation of humanity. These years brought Her from Her royal throne in heaven to earth. Here, She would intervene by simply teaching us to pray and depend on Her Son's loving grace for redemption and salvation. We shall tell the story of Her visits during that very troubled period in history to the remote field of Chousa Velha near the Village of Fátima where She appeared to three simple shepherd children to give them that most monumental message which would save mankind. This is the story of Our Lady of Fátima and The Bullet in Mary's Crown.

Mr. Francis Robert Roche, O.P., A.B.
(Brother Maurice Anthony)

The Angel of Peace in the sanctuary of Fatima

CHAPTER 1

An Angel Paves the Way 1915-1916

The sunny hillside near Aljustrel was perfect for grazing sheep. It was a hillside on Mount Cabeço near the hamlet of Aljustrel in the parish of Fátima where the bells of nearby St. Anthony's Church could be heard to summon the natives to pray the Marian prayer "terço" or third part of the Rosary each day. Four little girls said their Rosary: Maria Rosa Matias, her sister Teresa Matias, Maria Justino (from Casa Velha village), and Lùcia dos Santos from Aljustrel.

Suddenly, as they took their lunch, they saw a strange "cloud" whiter than snow hovering above the trees nearby with a very mysterious looking, transparent human form that they could not see clearly. Later, Lùcia reported this to her mother Maria Rosa Santos who then quickly dismissed this as "foolish girl's nonsense". Sometime much later in the year 1915, Lùcia saw the strange phenomenon again at the same place; and yet again a third time still later that year.

In the spring of 1916, while Lùcia and her two cousins, Jacinta and Francisco Marto were tending their flocks at nearby Chousa Velha, a field east of Mount Cabeço owned by Lucia's parents called Loco da Cabeço, an angelic vision of very dazzling splendor appeared. He began to speak very calmly to the three frightened children, *"Do not fear. I am the Angel of Peace. Pray with me."* Lùcia immediately began to recognize him as the vision she had seen dimly three times before; however, now he was radiantly clear though as transparent as crystal glass. He looked like a boy of 15 years old and wore a full-length robe. Though he floated in the air, he had no wings.

Lùcia de Jesus Santos was born on March 22, 1907 to Antonio and Maria Rosa dos Santos. She was then baptized at 7:00 p.m. on March 30, according to the register of St. Anthony parish of Fátima.

Francisco Marto was born June 11, 1908 and his sister, Jacinta Marto, on March 11, 1910. They were the youngest of a large family. Their mother, Olìmpia, had been married to Josè Fernandes Rosa for just over seven years with two sons, Antônio and Manuel (Rosa), before Josè died. Two years later, Olìmpia married Manuel Pedro Marto, and every year or so thereafter had another child.

Manuel Marto was 78 and Olìmpia 81 and in good health in 1950 when Father Joseph Pelletier visited them. Josè Marto was 81 and João (John) Marto was 74 when they were interviewed by Father Robert J. Fox in 1980.

These were indeed vigorous, hard-working country folks.

The Angel of Peace who had visited the three children lowered himself to the earth and then prostrated himself, as the people of the East pray, with his forehead to the ground saying,

"My God, I believe, I adore, I hope, and I love You. I implore Your pardon for those who do not believe, do not adore, do not hope, and do not love You."

This he repeated three times and the two girls joined him on the third; however, for reasons unknown, while Francisco could see clearly the vision and all the subsequent visions, he could not hear the sound of the angel's voice.

Little Jacinta had always been a very bright, bubbling chatterbox; but though she saw and heard everything, she knelt in complete silence before the visions. Subsequently the angel rose and said,

"Pray that way. The hearts of Jesus and Mary are attentive to your supplications."

Immediately he vanished leaving the children with their foreheads to the ground praying, "My God, I believe, I adore..." over and over again.

The children remained stunned and prostrate in a trance for some time barely conscious, repeating the prayer the angel taught them over and over again until they were exhausted. Their encounter with the angel was so profound, that they remained ecstatic for hours, later agreeing to discuss this unusual event only with each other.

Late that summer of 1916 came a particularly hot and dry season. The three children brought their flock of sheep that day to a shady spot near the well behind the dos Santos house to play where it was cooler for them and their animals. Suddenly, without warning the Angel of Peace appeared again and confronted them saying,

"What are you doing? Pray! Pray a great deal! The hearts of Jesus and Mary have designs of mercy on you. Offer prayers and sacrifices continually to the Most High."

Since Lùcia did not understand this request, she asked, "How are we to offer sacrifices? The angel replied,

"Make a sacrifice of everything you can, and offer it to the Lord as an act of reparation for the sins by which He is offended, and of supplication for the conversion of sinners. In this way draw peace upon our country. For I am its guardian angel, the Angel of Portugal. Above all, accept and bear with submission the suffering that the Lord will send you."

Finally, as abruptly as he came, the angel disappeared. The children were again paralyzed by the over powering and super naturalness of the angel's apparition. Francisco again saw the angel, but heard nothing. After Lùcia began to calm down, he asked Lùcia what the angel had said.

Lùcia, still overwhelmed replied, "I will tell you tomorrow morning. Today I just cannot talk."

And so poor Francisco waited patiently. The next morning, he went next door to the Santos house and immediately said, "Did you sleep last night? I've been wondering what the angel might have said to you."

Lùcia then told him everything the angel had said during the two apparitions. However, at only eight years of age, Francisco did not quite understand this. He was a normal boy in many respects, but he was not as intellectually gifted as either his cousin, Lucia, or his little "chatty" sister, Jacinta.

Francisco then asked Lùcia, "What is the Most High? And what is the meaning of 'The Hearts of Jesus and Mary are attentive to the voice of your supplications'?"

Being older, Lùcia tried her best to explain what she had heard. Still he didn't quite grasp these explanations, and had even more questions. She replied, "I'll tell you the rest later."

Little Jacinta, even though only six years of age and normally quite talkative, remained totally silent during all apparitions, indicating somewhat the depth of her awareness of what she was then experiencing. Of these angelic visits, the children agreed to tell no one; they discussed them in secret only among themselves as agreed.

* * *

After the second visit of the "Angel of Portugal," the three children daily spent hours meditating on the words of the angel while they attended their sheep as usual, their minds constantly reviewing the words of the angel to pray and offer sacrifices as they pondered their meaning.

Little Jacinta, the usually gregarious chatterbox, remarked to Lùcia, "I cannot speak, nor play, nor sing, and I haven't the strength to do anything. I don't know what is happening to me."

Her brother Francisco agreed, saying, "Nor have I. But what difference is it? The angel is more than all that; just think of him."

The three little shepherds then discussed the angel and the prayerful words he taught them, completely forgetting their usual games and barely remembering to eat their lunches.

"My God, I believe, I adore, I hope, and I love You. I implore Your pardon for those who do not believe, do not adore, de not hope, and do not love You."

In penitential reparation, they spent many long hours repeating the prayer with their foreheads to the ground, pausing only when their backs were racked with pain.

Weeks went by with the little shepherds saying the rosary, repeating the angelic prayer, and making many acts of mortification. Then, as suddenly as before, the angel appeared to them a third time in the fall of 1916 at the place where he had first appeared, the niche of the Loca do Cabeço. This time he carried in his left hand a radiant, magnificent chalice. In his right, he held above it a glowing host from which drops of blood fell into the chalice.

To quote Lùcia, "trazendo na mão un caliz e, sobre ele, uma hostias, da qual caiam dentro do caliz algumas gotas de sangue."

Leaving the chalice and host suspended in mid-air, the angel fell prostrate to the ground saying three times:

"Most Holy Trinity, Father, Son and Holy Spirit I adore You profoundly and offer You the most precious Body, Blood, Soul and Divinity of Jesus Christ, present in all the tabernacles of the earth, in reparation for the outrages, sacrileges, and indifference by which He Himself is offended. And by the infinite merits of His Most

*Sacred Heart and those of the Immaculate Heart of
Mary, I beg of You the conversion of poor sinners."*

The angel rose, took the host and chalice in his hands again, and placed the host on Lùcia's tongue. He gave the contents of the chalice to Francisco and Jacinta saying,

*"Take and drink the Body and Blood of Jesus Christ,
horribly outraged by ungrateful men. Make reparation
for their sins and console your God."*

For Lùcia there was the joy of receiving Holy Communion again; as for the two little siblings who had been anticipating their First Holy Communion, it was wonderful! Finally, having accomplished his task, the angel simply disappeared, never again to return.

Little Francisco had not heard the angel's voice and did not quite comprehend the meaning of what had happened. He turned to Lùcia and said, "The angel gave you Holy Communion, but what was it he gave to me and Jacinta?"

Before Lùcia could reply, astonished by her brother's lack of understanding, Jacinta spouted, "It was the same thing, Holy Communion! Didn't you see that it was the blood that dripped from the host?"

Because his extremely bright little sister's brief explanation satisfied him completely, he replied, "Now I understand. I did feel like God was in me, but I just didn't know how."

He knelt on the ground next to Jacinta; and the three prayed together for a while. They continued their prayers and sacrifices daily without fail, wondering what next would be in store for them. For what could the angel have been preparing them?

Spring time would soon be upon them; and the sheep must be moved from pasture to pasture to provide them succulent fresh grass. There was much work to be done; yet the three children also continued their fervent regimen of prayer and mortification, foregoing their old games and other pastimes, even their favorite games "Forfeits" and "Tag".

But little Jacinta's fondness for activities took hold and she suggested, "Let's build a wall around that bush over there. Lùcia and I will fetch the stones and you can make the wall."

Lùcia agreed, knowing the futility of opposing her little cousin's choice of "games". They would never dream what was to happen later at that bush.

The long dreary winter passed slowly. Nights were cold, though it does not snow on these lowlands, but only on the highest peaks of the great Serra da Estrella (Mountain Range of the Stars) which separates that part of Portugal from Spain far to the northeast of Aljustrel. Thirty miles to the west, past farms where rows and rows of vines draw nutrients from the alkaline soil to enrich their grapes for the finest wines, past many acres of the ugly cork trees whose bark becomes stoppers for the wine bottles, we find the Atlantic Ocean where two other industries flourish: fishing and tourism. Not very much had changed here for centuries; but as 1917 arrived, some things were about to change significantly.

Clockwise from top: Francisco, Lucia and Jacinta in front of the Holm Oak tree, Francisco, and Jacinta with Lucia

Our Lady of Fatima Church, Zacatecas City, Mexico

CHAPTER 2

The Lady of Light Arrives

The Côva da Iria is a pasture which belonged to Lùcia's father. It flowed northward with shady spots here and there. In early times the area was occupied by Muslims from Africa. While in their control, the village which is now St. Anthony of Padua parish, was controlled by these followers of the prophet Mohammed. The area was so lovely that they named it after his beautiful sister, Fátima. Even today, visitors are enthralled by this lovely region. Later in Christian times, the area just to the west became known as the Côva da Iria, probably named after St. Irene of Portugal (d. 653). It is to this spot that our story will draw our attention.

Following Sunday Mass, the children brought their flock to this lovely place which they loved. It was May 13, 1917 and the weather was simply beautiful. It was a perfect spring day to leave the animals grazing peacefully at the summit of the hill. Although winter is the raining season in Portugal, it is a prudent shepherd that keeps an eye out for the many sudden showers of springtime that are welcomed by farmers for the crops of wheat for bread, barley for beer, and grapes for wine. Although sheep, horses and goats can tolerate the rain, their little shepherds prefer to stay dry.

Meanwhile, the youngsters frolicked, prayed, and would at noon enjoy a picnic in the shade. Suddenly a bright flash of light lit up the Côva, causing Francisco to shout, "What was that?", to which Lùcia replied, "It must be lightning, yet it is strange that there are no clouds in the sky. Even so, there must be a storm beyond the hills. We had better get the sheep together and head for home."

Thoughts of lunch were quickly forgotten as plans changed; to get the animals down to the village before the storm was their new priority. They were experienced shepherds and they knew what to do.

The two little ones at once heeded her advice and helped move the flock southwest for Aljustrel. As they approached a "carrasqueira" tree where they had just played earlier, another very intense flash of light illuminated the sky as well as the entire countryside.

With blinking eyes, they prodded their flock to move faster down the hillside, when suddenly their pounding little hearts nearly stopped when they were caught in a brilliant, glowing light. There above the little tree, in dazzling light stood a beautiful young maiden.

She was dressed in a white luminous tunic with no collar or cuffs which fell to Her feet but was gathered in at Her waste with no belt or sash. A white mantle edged with a gold trim covered her head and flowed to Her feet exposing Her face, shoulders, hands and bare feet of flesh colored light at the front. Her hands, joined at Her breast in the posture of prayer, held a rosary with a white crucifix and beads which resembled pearls. Her feet rested on the top leaves of the sturdy car-rasqueira plant.

The children were frightened and in awe of this vision.

"Não tenhais medo. Eu não vos faço mal" (Don't be afraid, I won't harm you," She said, putting the children at ease.

"De onde e vossemecê?" (From where do you come?) Lùcia then inquired.

"Sou de Ceu" (I am from heaven) She replied.

Lùcia then asked, "E que è que Vossemecê me quer?" (What do you want of me?)

"Vim para vos pedir que venhais aqui seis meses se-guidos, no dia 13 à esta mêsma hora. Depois vos direi quem sou e o que quero. Depois voltarei ainda qaui uma sétima vêz." (I have come to ask you to come here for six months in succession, on the 13th day, at this same hour. Later on I will tell you who I am and what I want. Afterwards, I will return here yet a sev-enth time."

Lùcia and her little cousin, Jacinta, were sure right from the beginning that this visitor was none other than the Queen of heaven Herself. Her warm motherly voice put the children so much at ease that Lùcia proceeded to chat in a daughter/mother way. Again, as in the case of the angel who had prepared them for the arrival of Mary months earlier,

Jacinta remained silent in awesome respect and Francisco saw everything, yet heard nothing.

"E eu tambem vou para o Ceu?" Lùcia asked. (Will I also go to heaven?)

The Lady replied, "Sim, vais" (Yes, you will)

"E a Jacinta?" (and Jacinta?) Lùcia added.

"Ela Tambem", (she too) the Lady responded.

"E o Francisco?", Lùcia continued (and Francisco?)

"Tambem, mas tem que rezar muitos terços," (he too, but he must say many Rosarys).

At this point, Lùcia felt so comfortable talking to the vision, that she asked about friends who had died (perhaps during the then raging influenza epidemic). One was "Maria das Neves" who died at age 16 and the other an "Amelia" who had died at about age 18. The vision then informed Lùcia that Maria was in heaven, and that Amelia was in purgatory!

Then the Lady got profoundly serious saying,

> *"Quereis oferecer-vos a Deus para suportar todos os sofrimentos que Ele quiser enviar-vos, em acto de reparaçao pelos pecados com que Ele e ofendido e de suplica pela conversao dos pecadorers?" (Are you willing to offer yourselves to God and bear all the sufferings He wills to send you, as an act of reparation for the sins by which He is offended, and of supplication for the conversion of sinners?)*

"Sim queremos" (Yes, we are willing), she responded for the three of them.

"Ides, pois, ter muito que sofrer, mas a graça de Deus serão vôsso conforto". (Then you are going to have much to suffer, but the grace of God will be your comfort.)

Then She opened her hands wide communicating an intense light which penetrated the innermost depths of their souls.

World War I had been raging throughout Europe northeast of the Pyrenees Mountains which separated the Iberian Peninsula of Spain and Portugal from France. After a few moments She continued,

"Rezem o terço todos os dias para alcançarem a paz para o mundo e o fim da guerra" (Pray the Rosary every day in order to obtain peace for the world and an end to the war.)

She then rose serenely and disappeared into the vastness of space leaving the children with the awesome task of leading their country in prayer for protection from the horror of the devastating war and peace for their land.

* * *

The visits of the Angel of Peace had left the children simply exhausted; however, the motherly, affectionate and warm visit of the Lady was a joy which left them elated. While extremely happy, they had mixed feelings about their assignment which they had just accepted and Her warning of "much to suffer". Nevertheless, the three spent the rest of the afternoon talking about the vision and its joyful effect on them. The sunshine couldn't have been warmer, the gentle breeze so cool and enjoyable. Their state of happiness at having beheld the wonderful vision of the Lady from heaven kept them exuberant throughout the day. Even the animals behaved well!

Jacinta kept saying again and again, "Ai! Que Senhora tão bonita!" (Oh, what a beautiful Lady!)

Francisco also remarked that the brilliance of the light shining from Her was so strong that he had to lower his eyes downward. He asked question after question about what the Lady had said, for he could not heard Her voice just as he had not heard the voice of the angel who had previously visited them. Gabby little Jacinta was more than able to give him all the details. Again, they agreed to tell no one of the vision and the monthly visions which She had promised would come to them. They were not concerned as to why She was to make these visits. They were simply delighted that She was to return for more visits, for Her presence gave them a sense of joy that was most profound.

Later that afternoon when she arrived home, Lùcia told no one of the heavenly visitor as they had agreed. As always, after supper and evening prayers, she and her family went to bed. It had been a busy day for them all.

Farming in those days with no power tools, no electricity, and no running water made the basic things of life a very difficult series of tasks. Having large families provided the many hands that were needed to accomplish the daily work that had to be done; thus, most families had several children, each assigned his or her tasks. Everyone looked forward to a night of restful sleep.

At the Marto house, things were very different. Manuel and Olímpia Marto had gone to market to buy a pig and would not return until evening. Meanwhile, Francisco kept busy with yard work. Jacinta waited in the doorway for her parents' return from shopping.

When she caught sight of her mother, Jacinta ran up to her shouting, "Mother, Mother, I saw Our Lady at the Côva da Iria today!"

Olìmpia responded very skeptically, "My, my you must certainly be a good little girl to see Our Lady."

Jacinta then followed her into the kitchen insisting, "But I did see Her!" she cried.

"Nonsense, child," Olìmpia replied.

Whereupon Jacinta began to tell her everything that happened: the flash of lightning, their fear, the Lady surrounded by a blinding light asking them to say the Rosary every day.

At first Olìmpia dismissed the narrative saying, "You are very silly. As if Our Lady would appear to a little girl like you!"

After feeding the new pig, Manuel Marto joined his several children, his wife Olìmpia, and her brother Antònio da Silva for supper. When the meal was finished, and the dishes washed and put away, the family gathered by the warm glow of the fire in the hearth. Olìmpia then told little Jacinta to tell "her story" to the family.

The little one began quietly and with awesome simplicity and sincerity, "It was a Lady so very beautiful, so lovely, dressed in white." She then went on, "The Lady spoke a lot to Lùcia, but never to me or Francisco. I heard everything they said. The Lady told Lùcia that we must say the Rosary every day, and that She would take the three of us to heaven and many other things I don't know, but Lùcia does."

Francisco confirmed the words of Jacinta, and while the girls all seemed interested, the boys all laughed at the story, except their father, Manuel. He later admitted, "I believed what the children said was true almost at once. They had no education, not the least; they would never have thought of it."

The next morning, Olímpia told the "silly story" to some of her neighbors. It didn't take long for the news to spread down the street to Lùcia's family. First to hear was Maria dos Anjos, Lùcia's oldest sister who then inquired, "I have heard people talking, saying that you saw Our Lady at the Côva da Iria. Is that true?"

Lùcia was surprised saying, "Who told you that?" After a moment to compose herself she mumbled, "And I had asked her so much not to tell anyone!"

"Why?", inquired Maria dos Anjos.

"I don't know if it was Our Lady, but she was a most beautiful Lady," Lùcia replied.

Then Maria asked, "What did the Lady tell you?"

"She said She wanted us to go to the Côva da Iria for six months, without interruption, and then She would say who She is and what She wants."

Maria continued, "Did you ask Her who She was?"

"I asked Her where She was from; and She said to me, 'I am from Heaven' and...," Lùcia Santos said no more.

Francisco came along and confirmed Lùcia's suspicion that Jacinta had "talked". Her mother, Maria-Rosa Santos, laughed at the whole thing until her eldest daughter, Maria dos Anjos, confirmed what Lùcia had told her. The mother realized that something serious was taking place; and that spreading this "lie" would cause great scandal. She made Lùcia tell the whole story to her, yet she simply did not believe a word of it.

Little Jacinta was miserable and embarrassed because she had broken her promise to Lùcia, her best friend and closest cousin, of telling no one. The whole village seemed to laugh at them. The words of Our Lady, "You are going to suffer a great deal" began to unfold. Now they needed the "grace of God" to comfort them.

The three once joyful little shepherds were now quite miserable as they drove their flock to the Côva to graze the next day. Their state of depression was most profound.

The flowing tears of Jacinta had quickly dissolved the anger of Lùcia who had planned to scold her very soundly. The sweet little six-year-old begged for forgiveness; and it was quickly granted. At only ten years of age, Lùcia had exhibited maturity far beyond her actual years. She was the first choice of village families to look after their children when they were away on errands. Her ability to care for, amuse and entertain with games was extensive; and her petite cousin had intellectual capacity to match. They were constant companions. Both were reliable and completely dependable.

When the children reached the Côva da Iria on the afternoon of May 14, Jacinta sat on a rock with a look just as gloomy and down-trodden as ever. Lùcia felt so very sorry for her saying, "Jacinta, let us play!"

She responded, "I don't want to play today."

"Why not?" asked Lùcia.

"Because I am thinking that the Lady told us to say the Rosary and make sacrifices for the conversion of sinners. Now when we say the Rosary, we must say every word of the 'Hail Mary' and the 'Our Father'."

Previously, they had just said the word "Hail Mary" ten times. Lùcia agreed, saying, "Yes, but how are we going to make sacrifices?"

"We can give our lunch to the sheep," suggested Francisco; and indeed they did just that! At other times, however, they gave their lunches to other poor children whose families had barely enough to eat at evening supper. They ate bitter acorns, pine seeds and bell-flower roots as well as mulberries, raw mushrooms, and fruit from Lùcia's parents' nearby property.

The anger of their mothers who thought that this incident was just a fabricated story, a fairy tale, or an imagined daydream, made things difficult for the children. Within a day, the entire village of nine houses was bustling with gossip. Two weeks later Maria-Rosa received word from their pastor, Father Manuel Marquês Ferreira, that he wanted to see her and Lùcia at the St. Anthony's rectory in the town of Fátima of which Aljustrel was a village. The whole world seemed to be in turmoil.

While things seemed peaceful enough in the valley of Aljustrel, a horrible war was raging on the other side of the Pyrenees Mountains in France and beyond. The children of Fàtima knew little of this; yet the Virgin told them,

"Say the beads each day to obtain peace for the world and the end of the war."

The children were experiencing a somewhat different kind of war within their own village, yet their prayers were to apply to all sorts of conflict. They would be Her front line of defense for the free world as well. At about 8 degrees west longitude and 40 degrees north latitude, Portugal is the closest European country geographically to the North American continent across the Atlantic Ocean. Their prayers were to be for "peace for the world" coming from the heart and center of that little country.

Rotunda Santa Teresa de Ourem.

Lucia, Francisco and Jacinta

CHAPTER 3

The Trials Begin

In response to the pastor's request for an audience with them, Maria-Rosa and her daughter, Lùcia, attended Mass. Afterwards they made their way to the rectory. As they approached the veranda, Lùcia asked, "But Dear Mother, how can I say that I didn't see the Lady when I did see Her?"

Maria-Rosa kept silent since she didn't know what to respond. They sat on a bench in the hallway and waited for the pastor to return from the church.

The pastor, Rev. Manuel Marquês Ferreira, had heard various reports of the goings on at the village. He reviewed the many possibilities in his mind of what may have happened; of those there were several choices. If Our Lady had indeed appeared, She may be honoring Portugal as she did France at Lourdes in 1858. That would be a very great blessing for his parish and country. If it were simply a lie invented by the children to give themselves importance, that would be contrary to what he knew of them from his four years as the pastor. If it were an invention of their parents for vain glory and financial gain, it would be contrary to what he knew of both the Marto and Santos families who were devout church people and very hard-working farmers. It was also commonly known that Maria-Rosa vehemently did not believe the story and continually persecuted Lùcia whom she accused of lying. The fourth possibility was that of hallucination of a childish and pathological imagination; yet he knew of no history of any kind of family mental abnormality or sign of mental trouble.

The final possibility troubled the pastor deeply: a diabolical intervention. Yet why would the devil ask the children to pray the rosary?

The pastor entered the rectory and invited the two women to sit in his office. Father Ferreira spoke in a calm and amiable way and asked a number of questions. Many of the questions were adroitly worded to trap Lùcia in any kind of lie. When she replied with simple candor and not the slightest contradiction or disparity in her statements, he was very impressed. Maria-Rosa still screamed at her, "Now, Lùcia, admit to the pastor that it is all a lie!"

"But I can't say that it is a lie if it isn't," she replied.

"O Senhor Prior, see how obstinate she is. I have threatened her with all kinds of things if she continues to lie that she saw Our Lady, but I get absolutely nowhere with her."

The pastor then tried to calm Maria-Rosa who had become very agitated, "Come, come, my good woman. If what Lùcia has said is true, it is a great honor for her and for her family."

"Ah, yes, if it is true; but suppose it is a lie?" She retorted.

"Well, until it is proved to be a lie, I want you to treat your daughter as you were accustomed to doing before all this happened." With this, he dismissed the mother and child.

The three little shepherds continued to watch their flock each day in anticipation of the next visit of the heavenly Lady. June 13th would soon arrive, and She would have much more to say to them.

* * *

The gossip saying that monthly visits of the Virgin would happen on the thirteenth of each month had spread rapidly throughout the area and beyond. A number of people, about fifty of so, planned to join the children at the little carresqueira tree on the morning of June 13, 1917.

Upon their arrival at the Côva, the children and the group waited patiently. One sickly old woman from the nearby village of Moita, Maria Carreira, inquired of Lùcia, "my child, which is the tree where Our Lady appears?"

Lùcia obligingly replied, "See, this is where She stood" placing her hand over the top of the leafy branches of the stubby little tree.

Maria Carreira was a believer right from the beginning and became known as "Maria da Capelina" (Mary of the Little Chapel). She had been given up by her doctors who said that she had only a short time to live due to the gravity of her illness. In spite of that, she kept herself busy clearing the area around the bush, having a little chapel built, and doing daily visits there to honor the Virgin. Though she was never cured, she had continued to live for years, and many decades later told of her experiences of the many things she had witnessed to Father John de Marchi, IMC, from her bed in the Fátima Shrine Hospital which had been built many years after the 1917 events.

Since it was nearly noon, many opened their picnic boxes and began to eat their lunches. Some offered food to the children, but the most they would accept was an orange. Since there was little shade, and Maria's strength was fading in the hot June sun, she asked, "Will Our Lady be much longer in coming?"

"No senhora, she will not be long in coming," was Lùcia's reply as she began to lead them in the recitation of the Rosary. Upon finishing, a girl from Boleiros started the Litany, but Lùcia stopped her saying, "There is no time for that now."

She rose to her feet, arranged her shawl and white kerchief saying, "Jacinta, there comes Our Lady now."

Everyone fell to their knees as a very brilliant flash of lightning startled the group.

The children quickly became enraptured by what only they could see; yet many said they could hear a buzzing sound in response to Lùcia's questions. Besides the flash of lightning, everyone noticed a grey "mist" floating around the base of the holm-oak bush. There was no doubt in anyone's mind that something mystical was happening.

Lùcia raised her eyes upward and asked again as she did during the first visit, "O que me quer vossemeçe?" (What do you want of me?) Everyone heard Lùcia's voice; however, though Maria Carreira and the others strained to hear a response, they heard only that very faint sound like the buzzing of a bee. Francisco heard Lùcia's voice, but as earlier, he could only see the Lady and so he struggled to read Her lips.

The heavenly Lady said to Lùcia, "I want you to come here on the thirteenth of each month, and to recite the beads every day. I desire that you learn to read. Later I will tell you what else I want."

Lùcia remembered a petition she had been asked to transmit saying, "There is a cripple who has asked that you cure him."

And the vision replied, "Tell him that if he converts himself, he will be cured within a year."

Pleased with this reply, Lùcia said, "I would like to ask you to take us to heaven."

"Yes, I will take Jacinta and Francisco in a short while, but you are to remain here on earth for some time longer. Jesus wants to use you to make Me known and loved and to establish in the world devotion to My Immaculate Heart. To those who embrace it, I promise salvation."

"Am I to remain here alone?" she asked.

"No my daughter, I will never abandon you. My Immaculate Heart will be your refuge and the way that will lead you to God."

With these words, the vision began to float away.

"Look! There She goes," shouted Lùcia. While only the three children could see Her, many heard a sound like the rumble of an explosion coming from beneath the tree. Maria Carreira said the light, cloud-like smoke rose from the tree with a noise like a rocket taking off flowing in the direction to which Lùcia pointed. The vision ended.

The two-dozen people who had witnessed these phenomena were filled with many questions to ask. "Was it really Our Lady? What did She look like? What did She wear? What did She say?"

Lùcia's brief answers were carefully worded: "Our Lady said to recite the beads. She told us to remain here on the thirteenth day of next month. And she wants us to learn to read." The inquisitive spectators asked for more, but Lùcia evasively replied, "Yes, but it is a secret."

They all then returned to the village praying and singing along the way. When they arrived at their village, the procession in honor of the feast of St. Anthony was under way. Their joyful singing made many wish they had gone to the Côva as well for something wonderful surely must have happened. The three little shepherds, however, spent the rest of the day pondering the momentous message that the Lady from heaven had given them that day. Why several more visits? What more would She reveal to them? And what was the significance of Her coming always on the thirteenth of each month? There seemed to be more questions than answers She had given them.

She had promised heaven soon for Francisco and Jacinta and later for Lùcia; but what hardships must they endure now? Things were already very difficult at home with all the abuse they were receiving from family and neighbors.

Would She keep Her promise to Lùcia?

The Bullet in Mary's Crown

*"I will never leave you. My Immaculate Heart will be
your refuge and the way that will lead you to God."*

Both Francisco and Jacinta were pleased with the results of the second visit, for Our Lady had told them the good news that they would go to heaven. Still Lùcia was filled with questions. How long must she stay on earth to serve the Lady? What must she do to render this service? What is the significance of Her visiting them monthly on the thirteenth of each month? Why not any other day? What more would She reveal to them the next time She came?

Little Francisco who had enjoyed playing tunes on his wooden flute and occasionally "football" (soccer) with his friends, took Her words to heart, "He must say many Rosaries." He stopped going to school, became somewhat withdrawn and could be found alone in the village church near the altar with his rosary in one hand and his other against the bronze tabernacle door as he whispered his prayers to the hidden Jesus inside.

The children could hardly wait for July 13th to arrive. Their days tending their flock seemed to be endless during that long hot summer. Many things may have been the same at the village, but other things were definitely not. Many began to "believe", but many others derided them and treated them badly. Perhaps in July the Lady would give them the help they so desperately needed. The stress of waiting was too much for her; and finally, on July 12th, Lùcia told her cousins that she would simply not go to the Côva again. They must go alone!

The road to Ajustrel

CHAPTER 4

The Third Apparition
&
Mary's Many Other Visits Elsewhere

O n the morning of Friday, July 13th, dozens of people from villages, towns and distant places, including pious believers, curious unbelievers, and inquiring skeptics responded to the sensational anticlerical press that had spread the news far and wide without intending to promote religion, but to deride it. The dirt roads leading to the Côva were lined with people coming from all directions.

Lùcia had decided not to go that day; yet after pondering the situation, she went to the Marto house nearby and found the two little ones in their bedroom crying bitterly. "Well, aren't you going to the Côva" she asked?

"We don't dare go without you. But come, Lùcia, come with us!" Their tears changed to joyful smiles. They jumped to their feet as Francisco exclaimed, "I am so glad you are going

35

to the Côva. I didn't sleep at all last night. I spent the whole time crying and praying that Our Lady would make you go."

It seemed that nearly their whole village was going. Both Manuel Pedro and Olímpia were among the hundreds already there when the children arrived. Maria Carreira had brought her family, including her seventeen-year-old crippled son, João, in the hope of a cure for him. Others had come earlier and placed poles with lanterns above the holm-oak bush. There was a sense of hope for change of their situations.

The Communists had taken over the government of many cities to the south; but the heavily populated Catholic oriented northern cities had resisted vehemently. Hope for them had been gradually waning yet something "new" was about to happen. As Lùcia, Francisco and Jacinta knelt to begin the Rosary, thousands joined them, beads began to appear amongst the large crowd. As one observer noted, "...in between dainty manicured fingers, rough cracked hands, and hard calloused fists."

Almost immediately Lùcia was blinded by the bright flash of light that always announced the arrival of their Visitor. Many had used umbrellas to shade themselves from the very intense midday sunshine, so Lùcia shouted, "Close your umbrellas. The Lady is already coming... there!"

In the center of dazzling light as in the first two apparitions was the beautiful Lady from heaven. Lùcia was somewhat embarrassed by her original reluctance to be there that day.

Realizing that She would know this, she was enheartened by Her gracious attitude; again she asked, "O que e que vossemeçe me quer hoje?" (What do you want of me today?)

The Lady replied,

"I want you to return here on the thirteenth of the coming month and to pray the terço every day to honor Our Lady of the Rosary to obtain peace for the world and the end of the war, for she alone can help you."

Lùcia then courageously said, "I would like to ask You to tell us who You are. And would You perform a miracle so that everyone will believe that You are appearing to us."

In response to this request, the Virgin said,

"Continue to come here every month. In October, I will tell you who I am and what I want. And I will perform a miracle which all shall see in order that they may believe."

Having brought dozens of requests with her, Lùcia then petitioned the Virgin for these needy, blind, crippled and sickly folks. Requests were from the Correira family, a dying man in Atouguia, and the like.

To these requests, She replied,

"João Correira will either be cured or given means for gaining his livelihood within a year. He too must say the beads with his family. The man from Atouguia should not be in a hurry to die: I know best when to come for him."

Other requests were also answered. The Virgin then opened Her hands and showed the children a vision of a sea of hell fire with devils and human lost souls wailing with cries of pain and floating like glowing embers. The children turned pale with fright, and Lùcia screamed, "Oh... Our Lady!"

Our Lady explained:

"You have seen hell where the souls of poor sinners go. To save them, God wants to establish throughout the world devotion to My Immaculate Heart. If people do what I tell you, many souls will be saved and there will be peace. The war is going to end. But if they do not stop offending God, another even worse war will break out during the reign of Pius XI. When you see a night that is illuminated by an unknown light, know that it is a sign that God gives you that He is going to punish the world for its crimes by means of war, hunger, and the persecution of the Church and the Holy Father."

"To forestall this, I shall come to ask for the consecration of Russia to My Immaculate Heart and the Communion of Reparation on the first Saturdays. If My requests are heeded, Russia will be converted and there will be peace; otherwise she will spread her errors throughout the world promoting many wars, persecution of the Church, many good will be martyred, the Holy Father will suffer much, and various nations will be annihilated. But in the end, My Immaculate Heart will triumph. And the Holy Father will consecrate Russia to Me and be converted. Then some time of peace will be given the world. In Portugal, the dogma of the faith will always be preserved. Tell this to no one except Francisco."

Lùcia then asked, "Do you want anything else from me?"

And She replied,

"No, today I desire nothing else from you."

With this final remark, the Virgin departed with a sound that made the lanterns shake on the arch that had been built. The grey mist floated away and for a moment there was silence.

The crowd swept inward with many questions, for they had seen the facial expressions of horror that the children had exhibited during the vision. "What did the Lady say to make you so sad?"

"No, I cannot tell it," Lùcia replied.

With that, Jacinta's father lifted her into his arms, his hat shading her from the intense sun, Francisco was swept up into the arms of another relative, and Lùcia was carried on the shoulders of a very tall man. The very joyful entourage departed the Côva and returned to Aljustrel.

The very happy retinue of several hundred happy pilgrims had experienced something truly wonderful that left them singing and praying all the way home. The three little ones, however, were serious and silent, for they alone had seen a vision of hell which they would keep secret for a long time.

* * *

The visits of the Virgin Mary to the children at Fátima are often considered unique, yet the Queen of Heaven has made many visits to the world, the most documented of these have been listed in Appendix B. There is always a reason for Her to come to earth. That reason is usually simply to bring mankind to God. A few examples will show the power of Her influence for the good of mankind.

In 1531 near what is now Mexico City, Mary appeared to a 57-year-old Aztec widower named Juan Diego who had been made a Christian by Franciscan friars who came with the Spanish "conquistadors" to Central America. For many centuries, the pagan Indians had worshiped an evil idol," Quetzalcoatl," a serpent with feathers or flying serpent. Images of this god are found on many of the pyramids of Mexico. This serpent was actually a comet that appeared in the sky periodically that they thought was a serpent of fire. To appease the serpent, they made thousands of bloody human sacrifices each year in a futile attempt to keep him away; but he returned regularly every few years. The friars had learned their Nahautl language, and then explained how the invisible true God became man, was named Jesus and gave his own life on a cross to save all men for all time.

This new religion made sense to them who heard this and they were converted as was Juan Diego; however, Mary wanted the entire Aztec nation to be converted and the killing stopped.

Mary appeared to Juan Diego on Saturday morning, the 9th of December, as he made his way to Mass in honor of Our Lady at the church of Santiago in Tlaltellolco village.
She told him to tell the bishop-elect Franciscan Juan de Zumarraga to build a great "temple" on Tepeyac Hill next to a dried-up lake. Upon hearing this, the bishop thought the idea was foolish, and asked Diego to get proof that the Virgin was really making this request.

When Diego next saw Mary, he asked for a proof to bring to the bishop. She told him to bring a bouquet of the flowers growing in the snow nearby. It was winter, yet at that high altitude, Diego found roses growing in the snow. These Castilian roses that normally only grow in Spain would surely convince the bishop. Diego spread his tilma (cloak) on the ground, filled it with roses, carefully rolled up the bundle, and brought them down to bishop's office. Although Friar Zumarraga was in the middle of a meeting, Juan in his excitement, burst into the room unannounced. He held the tilma up to drop the roses onto the floor; the friars all gasped! It was not for the flowers that they reacted, but because they beheld a life-size image of Our Lady on the tilma. While Juan had been on his way to the bishop, he had stopped to visit his dying uncle, Juan Bernadine, who told him that he had just been miraculously cured by the Virgin Mary using the Nahautl phrase "te coatlaxopeuh". This sounded like the name of the Spanish place, "Guadalupe". [The Nahautl actually means: Te (stone), coa (serpent), tla (the), xopeauh (crush).] The image of Mary shows Her foot crushing the head of a serpent. Later when the natives saw this, they joyfully converted by the thousands each week to Christianity, for they understood this kind of hieroglyphic picture writing. These Aztec/Spanish people are the Mexicans of today. Juan Diego died in 1548 at 74 years of age.

It should also be noted that in 1962 during a careful examination by a team of scientists, a greatly enlarged photo of the eyes of the image on the tilma shows three people in the pupil kneeling before Her: perhaps Juan Diego, his uncle, and maybe bishop Zumarraga! The rough cactus fiber of which the tilma is made should have rotted away in 15 to 20 years, yet it is still on display at Mexico City Cathedral in a glass case above the altar after more than 500 years. Scientists and artists claim that the fabric is too rough to paint on, yet the image remains bright, clear and intense. A bombing on November14, 1921 by anti-religious fanatics and later the accidental spilling of nitric acid by a silversmith who was cleaning the frame have not ruined it.

Just as Our Lady of Guadalupe held Her hands folded in prayer, so did She at Fátima, an angel appearing at Her feet! Perhaps it was this angel that in 1830 brought Sister Catherine Labourè at midnight to the convent chapel of Saint Vincent de Paul in Paris to meet Mary who was waiting for her there. Mary wore 15 gold rings which at that time was popular in France instead of a Rosary of chained beads. The rings represented the 15 mysteries of the Rosary. Mary asked that an oval shaped metal be struck with Her image on one side and a "M" with a cross and twelve stars on the reverse side. This could be pinned to clothing to remind folks to say the Rosary. Saint Catherine was canonized in 1947.

Still later in 1846, Mary appeared further southeast in the French diocese of Grenoble just south of the Swiss border and west of the Italian border at the tiny village of La Salette. She appeared to two young shepherds who had just met that afternoon while grazing their herds of cattle on the hillside. Melanie Matthieu, age 15, and Maximin Giraud, age 11, came upon "a beautiful lady" sitting on a rock in the bed of a dried-up stream. She wore a crown and was weeping. Her message to the two youngsters was of a dire punishment for the human race if it did not repent of missing Mass, cursing, and sinfulness. It would include famines, earthquakes, and epidemics of mortal illness. This dire message was then relayed to the Holy See.

Later on, to the far southwest, near the Spanish border, to the village of Massabielle near Lourdes, our Lady appeared to 14-year-old Bernadette Soubirous fourteen times in 1858. Her message was to confirm the 1854 dogma of the Immaculate Conception by saying to Bernadette on March 25, the Feast of Annunciation,"Je suis Le Conception Immaculè". (I am the Immaculate Conception) Young Bernadette was somewhat retarded, and other children would not play with her. She had amused herself by playing alone on the outer edge of the village at what was the village dump. It was there that Mary visited her. instructed her to manually dig a hole from which water began to spring and which now emits 27,000 gallons daily. Thousands of infirm people come here annually, touch the water and are cured. Since 1884, a medical bureau of several hundred doctors of all faiths (and a few of no faith) examine thousands of patients. Only if no other possible natural or medical explanation is possible do they deem a cure to be miraculous. Again Mary asked for a church to be built and the Basilica of the Holy Rosary was completed in 1901, replacing a little chapel that had served until then.

At Pontmain just 30 miles from Laval, France, Mary visited Joseph (age 10) and Eugene (age 12) Barbette at 5:30 p.m. on January 17, 1871. Within minutes other children joined them. Only the children saw the vision. Although the adults, including a teaching Sister from the nearby convent, could not see the vision, they observed the children's happy reaction to what they could see. Knock, Ireland (1879); Fátima, Portugal

(1917); Beauraing, Belgium (1932); Banneaux, France (1933), the list continues. She is always guiding, constantly teaching, and diligently protecting humanity, Her children. At Fátima, when Mary appeared six times on the 13th of each month, She usually included the words of warning that "the Holy Father will have much to suffer" in some sort of catastrophe to come. Was a disaster to happen on the13th of a future month and in what year? Why could She not be more specific? Could it be that prophesy must be shrouded in mystery for only a few to understand since clearly predicting the future (fortune telling) was forbidden by Jewish law, and Mary was a "perfect" Jew in every way. For many generations the prophets of old had dealt with this problem by their mystical writing techniques which only a few "learned" people could decipher.

In ages past, Mary's visits had dealt with the here and now of that time. But at Fátima, Her message in the early twentieth century would deal with the now and of future time yet to come. Though She chose three of the littlest of shepherds to convey Her most awesome message, She would punctuate the delivery with the grandest of miracles to astound thousands who would witness the event.

Homes of the Marto and Santos families

Arturo de Oliveira Santos, the mayor of Ourem, who had the Fatima seers kidnapped and imprisoned in August 1917, threatening the children with execution if they did not reveal the Secret of the Virgin Mary told to them

CHAPTER 5

Kidnapped and Politics

The first three appearances of the Virgin Mary had made a great disturbance in the community of Fátima which belonged to Oúrem County. The Chief County Magistrate was a man named Artur Oliveira Santos whose family had him baptized in the Catholic faith as a child. He gave up the faith at age twenty to join the Masonic Lodge of Leiria. He then founded a lodge at Oúrem, and published a local newspaper which strived to undermine the faith of the people in the priests and the Church. This had made him a powerful political figure who wanted to crush the growing religious fervor that had been very rapidly developing throughout the country. Arturo de Oliveira Santos, mayor of Oúrem, had the seers kidnapped and imprisoned in August 1917. He threatened them with execution by boiling in oil if they would not reveal the "secret" the Virgin Mary told them. They stood firm and refused to reveal anything to him and finally had to be released.

While many citizens feared this powerful Magistrate, one man stood boldly and fearlessly against him for the good of his children, his family and the Church. This man was Jacinta's father, Manuel Pedro Marto. Although he was an uneducated man who could neither read nor write, he very well understood the evil of Communism that was trying to overtake his country. His deep intelligence could be found even in his youngest offspring, little Jacinta.

The two fathers of the children had been summoned to appear at noon with Lucia to the County House. Once they had arrived for the appointment, the Magistrate, who didn't know that there were three children involved, shouted at "Tio" Marto, "Where is the boy?" Marto was not at all intimidated, and simply shrugged his shoulders.

The angry Magistrate then asked Antônio Santos, Lùcia's father, "Do the people of Fátima believe in these things?" Santos timidly answered. "Not at all. All that is just women's talk."

Then the Magistrate turned to "Tio" Marto, "And you?"

"Tio" Manuel Marto replied boldly, "Yes, sir, I do believe it is true what they say."

To this the Magistrate simply laughed and then he dismissed Lùcia admonishing her that she must tell him the "secret" he had heard about or die. Lùcia remained silent. This short meeting with the Magistrate accomplished nothing for him, but left everyone agitated and uneasy. The families then returned to their village.

On Monday, August 13th, when Tio Marto arrived home after hoeing his garden, he found the Magistrate waiting in the parlor and said, "So you are here!"

To this the Magistrate replied, "Yes, of course, I want to see the miracle, too."

In his heart Tio Marto sensed something was wrong when the Magistrate offered to take them in his carriage and stop at the rectory to see the pastor. Marto did not trust him at all. Even Father Ferreira seemed to have changed his mind regarding the matter from believing to thinking the children had probably made up the story after all.

At the rectory he asked, "Who taught you to say the things you are going about saying?"

Whereupon Lùcia replied, "The Lady whom I saw at the Côva da Iria."

The pastor warned her that liars go to hell and that she must tell the truth. He then asked, "Is it true that the Lady confided a secret to you?"

"Yes, but I can't tell it. If Your Reverence wants to know it, I shall ask the Lady for permission to tell it to you (when we see Her today)." Lùcia carefully said "the Lady" and not "Our Lady" as the woman in the vision had not yet identified Herself, but had promised to do so later "in October".

Since the Magistrate had no intention of actually going to the Côva, he interrupted saying, "Let's be on our way."

Once in the carriage again, he set the horse in rather rapid motion, and Lùcia shouted, "This is not the way to the Côva da Iria!"

People along the roadway realized that the Magistrate was kidnapping the children and they began to stone him, so he then covered the children with a cloak until they reached his house. Once inside, he locked them in a room saying, "You won't leave this room until you tell me the secret."

Soon thereafter, the Magistrate's kind wife took the children from the room, gave them a good lunch, and let them play with her own children reading picture books. Perhaps she had hoped that a softer approach would get to the truth. Still, nothing changed their testimony.

The three were then interrogated separately by the Magistrate and threatened to be boiled in oil if each did not tell the truth. In spite of all these threats they stood firm, ready to die. Finally, since he got nowhere with them, he returned them to their homes on the morning of August 15th. The very large crowd that had gone to the Côva on the 13th saw lightening and other types of phenomena as before, but in the absence of the three little shepherds, these phenomena ended quickly.

After being released, Lùcia, Francisco and his older brother, John, went to a different meadow called Valinhos with their flock of sheep. The reason they had gone to Valinhos is that the many hundreds of people that had been going to the Côva da Iria had ruined the grass there, leaving a muddy mess. Although it was two days "late," Lùcia sensed that the Lady was coming while they were at Valinhos and bribed John with coins to go and get Jacinta, one coin now and another when they returned. As soon as the little one arrived, Our Lady appeared. She promised again a great miracle in October and added Her request that two "litters" be made, one to be carried by Lùcia, Jacinta and two other girls, and the other by Francisco and three other boys to collect funds for a chapel to be built. This had been a custom for many years to raise funds for the needy and the poor at festival times.

Lùcia then requested cures for a number of people, and the Lady responded,

"Yes, I will cure some of them during the year. Pray, pray very much and make sacrifices for sinners, for many souls go to hell because they have no one to pray and make sacrifices for them."

As before, She began to leave the children by ascending toward the east into a cloud with the gentle rumble of thunder. Here at Valinhos She had also made Her appearance standing on a Holm-oak bush, so Lùcia took a branch which gave off a wonderful odor of sweet perfume to bring home with her for her mother Maria-Rosa who was delighted by the aroma which filled the room when Lùcia entered.

The three children had been severely depressed by having been kidnapped, ruthlessly interrogated by the Magistrate, cross-examined by the pastor and then missing their original August 13th appointment with their heavenly visitor. Mary had warned them that they would have much to suffer as events would unfold, and it was all happening to them just as She had foretold. Yet Her surprise visit on the 15th filled them with happiness again, for She was keeping Her promise to Lùcia,

"My daughter, I will never abandon you."

Our Lady had missed them among the thousands waiting at the Côva, but She had found them alone at Valinhos.

* * *

An enormous crowd of an estimated eighteen thousand people that had gathered at the Côva da Iria on August 13, 1917 had witnessed the usual clap of gentle thunder, the small cloud of mist surrounding the holm-oak bush, and the soft glow of light as had been seen earlier. Still there was even more to behold.

According to Maria da Capelina, "Looking about, everyone's face glowed rose, red, blue, all the colors of the rainbow. The trees seemed all covered with flowers. Our clothes. also into rainbow colors. The two vigil lanterns hanging from the arch appeared to be of gold. When these signs disappeared, the people seemed to realize that Our Lady had come, and, not finding the children, had returned to heaven."

When word arrived a few moments later that the Magistrate had taken the children, the crowd became an angry mob set on going to Oùrem to protest. Tio Marto had gone to the Côva after the children had been taken hostage, realized that he must intervene to avoid harm to the Magistrate and the pastor whom they considered guilty.

To be heard above the tumult of the crowd, he shouted in a loud voice, "Be calm, men, be calm. Do not hurt anyone. Whoever deserves punishment will get it by the power of the One above."

The underhanded action of the Magistrate to stop at the rectory to further interrogate the children on their way to the Côva had embarrassed the pastor. Because he did not know of the Magistrate's alternate plan to take them to Oùrem, he wrote a letter to the newspapers which was published a few days later. It read, in part: "The rumor that I was an accomplice to the sudden kidnapping of the children... I repel as an unjust and insidious calumny. The Magistrate did not confide the secret of his intentions to me."

Although the entire text is a full page long, it reached few people to whom it was directed, since most villagers were

illiterate and did not buy or read newspapers. Despite his inno-
cence, Father Ferreira never again regained the confidence of
the people and was soon transferred out of Fátima parish by
the bishop.

In 1910, the "free-thinkers and anti-clericals," now re-
ferred to as "communists," shot and killed the Catholic Portuguese king and crown prince as their motorcade arrived in Lisbon. They seized power and established what they called a "republic". Though he was only twenty-six years old and had just
a meager education, Artur de Oliveira Santos had been selected
to be the Administrator of the Vila Nova de Oùrem District,
Municipal Council president, and the Deputy District Judge.

Together with the local newspaper which he owned,
Artur became the most influential and feared man in the entire
district with virtual dictatorship over the area which included
Fátima which is within Vila Nova da Oùrem. He was both
feared by most and hated by all. His only real training was as a
tinsmith, and he was often called by many, "O Estanheiro,"
the Tinsmith.

With the complete separation of Church and State, the
Communists had planned to eradicate the Church in just one
or two generations. One government after another failed. They
had not anticipated the power of a heavenly Queen who would
hold the nation together. Then came Salazar.

Antônio de Oliveira Salazar was an economics professor who was born in 1889 at Beiro Alto in Lisbon, Portugal.
His parents had sent him to a seminary to become a priest; but
after 8 years of study, at age 18, he left the seminary. Then in
1910 at age 21 he enrolled at the very prestigious University of
Coimbra and earned a degree in economics. Since his student

*Antonio de Oliveira Salazar
(1940)*

performance had been quite outstanding, he received an academic appointment there and was eventually made a professor in 1918. Salazar wrote very extensively on political economy, gave many speeches, and was elected in 1921 to the national legislature. As finance minister he demanded and received control of the government, balanced the budget, brought financial prosperity to the country, and in 1932 became the president of the Council of Ministers which ruled Portugal. The Church was then guaranteed religious freedom when in 1933 he created the "Estado Novo," a corporatist state which adhered to a system of social justice that in 1915 had been promulgated by the papal encyclical "Rerum Novarum" of Pope Benedict XV.

Salazar ruled Portugal as a benevolent dictator for the next three and a half decades. He kept his country neutral during war times, preserving 700 years of cultural beauty from the devastation of wars. In 1968 he suffered a stroke, and died in 1970, but not before advising his cabinet to "look to America" and produce a government with all the good qualities that give its people "a good life of freedom".

Within hours, a new Socialist-Republic was then formed with a presidential five-year term limited to one second term and a unicameral parliament of elected regional representatives based on population serving similar terms.

Freedom of religion was guaranteed. More than 90 percent of the citizens currently declare that they are Catholics, though less than half the population attends Mass regularly. As in all free countries, the younger generation takes their freedom for granted, often forgetting the true source of freedom. "Know the Truth, and Truth will set you free. I am the Way, the Truth and the Life, Christ Jesus."

The older generations of Portuguese remember that their freedom and national security were brought about by a "seminary drop-out" who had never lost his faith in God or his country.

The Queen of Heaven's influence endures.

King Carlos I

The coat of arms of Portugal

CHAPTER 6

Great Throngs of Thousands Trek to Fatima

Without the benefit of radio, television or "free" newspapers, the word about the "Tinsmith" and his brutal failed attempt to force the children to recant their story of a Lady from heaven spread throughout the land. Soon multitudes of skeptics or hesitants became convinced and transformed into believers. Thousands of people from far and wide, from villages, towns and places of great distance, took time off from their many important duties for as much as two or three days to make the trek on dusty, unpaved roads to the Côva da Iria. It was a great ordeal. And it was dangerous. Yet there were great dangers elsewhere.

While returning from the palace of Vila da Viconsa to Lisbon in an open carriage, the Royal family, King Carlos I (1863-1908), his wife Queen Marie Amelia, Prince Luis Filipe (1887-1908, and young Prince Manõel II (1889-1932), shots were fired by two republican activists, Alfredo Costa and Manuel Buica, as the royal carriage passed through the Terreiro do Paço near the waterfront. The three royal men were hit. The king died instantly, Prince Luis Philipe died 20 minutes later after being taken to the nearby Navy Arsenal. Prince Manõel was hit in the arm but survived. The queen was not injured. The two assassins were killed on the spot by the body guards and police. Prince Manõel though only eighteen was then proclaimed king and served for two years. The two political parties, the Regenerators and the Progressists, were deeply divided neither party leader appearing in the cabinet and members at odds with each other. On young King Manõel's return from his summer home in Bucaço, revolution broke out and the Lisbon palace was shelled. Manõel first fled to the National Palace in Mafra and then into exile in England. Then the Republic of Portugal was proclaimed upon his abduction in 1910.

Manõel settled in London and later in Twickenham where on September 4, 1913 he married the daughter of Prince Wilhelm of Hohenzollern, Augusta Victoria, and devoted himself to book collecting and published "Early Portuguese Books, 1489-1600" a three-volume set (1929). He died on July 2, 1932. They had no children.

Then communists began their work taking over the larger cities of Portugal. Many city folk no longer went to church for fear of a similar fate as their king. Only in remote villages and towns was religion openly practiced. But this was soon to change for the Queen of Heaven had Her plan.

To Fàtima people came from all directions, feet swollen and sore from miles of plodding through rough trails and stony country roads. Many traveled with donkeys dragging litters with their sick or crippled, their tiny children in their arms, or packages of food and supplies balanced on their heads. Hundreds were praying the Rosary aloud; others joyfully singing favorite hymns which echoed over the hills of the countryside. Others used horse-drawn carriages or their new-fangled "motor cars". All were headed for the Côva.

The Magistrate ("The Tinsmith") had sent government troops to block the roads but they vainly tried to send the people away, often chasing them into the fields. The troops were simply overwhelmed by the sea of an estimated 30,000 people that had come and filled the huge bowl-shaped Côva. By late morning on Thursday, September 13, there was an ocean of humanity present. Most were prayerful believers, but there were also a few of those with simple curiosity. A good many who had not held rosaries for years in their fingers worn by hard work and age, now fervently counted the Hail Marys. These were a mix of the wealthy, the poor, city folks and the mountaineers, all in expectation of a wonderful happening.

There were also several men in black suits in various places throughout the crowd. Among them were a number of curious seminarians as well as the well-known priests Rev. Joao Quaresma, Rev. Manuel do Carmo Gois, Rev. Manuel Pereira da Silva and, most notably, the Rev. Dr. Manuel Nunes Formigão, professor at the seminary and lyceum of Santarem. Father Formigão would become a key figure in the story of Fàtima.

At noon, the bells of St. Anthony's church began to peal the Angelus and the glow of the sun in the cloudless sky began to diminish. A globe of light began to advance from east to west causing thousands of arms to point in the direction of the advancing glow with many shouting, "Look, look, it's beautiful..."

Father Quaresma turned his head and said, "Yes, I can clearly see a globe of light moving toward the children." Then Father Carmo Gois added, "I see it too."

As the large throng of spectators gazed in awe, a shower of brilliant, glowing flower-like petals began to fall from the cloudless sky. Many reached up to grab them, but the glistening globules simply disappeared just above their heads. The children had dropped to their knees, for Our Lady was present before them and She remained silent for a few moments.

Lùcia began the conversation with her usual question, "O que e que vossemece me quer?" (What do you want of me?)

The Lady then replied,

"Continue to say the beads so as to bring about the end of the war. In October, Our Lord will come, as will Our Lady of Sorrows, and Our Lady of Mount Carmel. Saint Joseph will also come with the Child Jesus to bless the world."

The Lady paused for a moment and with a warm facial expression and great tenderness in Her voice continued, *"God is pleased with your sacrifices, but He does not want you to sleep with the rope. Wear it only during the day."*

Lùcia was very flattered by this, lowering her eyes in a soft blush. Then raising her eyes again, Lucia began to list many petitions and requests that folks had given her.

"I will cure some of them within a year, but not the others," was Her reply.

Recalling that Maria Carreira (da Capellina) and other pious folks were anxious to build the chapel requested by the Lady the previous month at Valinhos with money they had raised, Lùcia then inquired, "Would you like a little chapel built here (at the Côva) with the money people have given?"

To this the Lady responded, "Yes, I would like a little chapel built here in honor of Our Lady of the Rosary. But tell the people to use only half of the money for the new chapel. The other half should be used for the cult and feast of Our Lady of the Rosary. Two processional biers should be made with the money and the remainder of it carried on these biers to the parish church during the festivities in honor of Our Lady of the Rosary. You and Jacinta and two other girls carry one; Francisco and three other boys carry the other."

It should be noted that collection of funds this way was an ancient tradition to obtain means to support various activities including the purchase of food for the poor during festivals throughout the year.

Lùcia then turned her attention to a more personal problem saying, "There are many who say that I am an impostor and deserve to be hanged and burned. Please perform a miracle so that all will believe."

The Lady then repeated Her promise,

"Yes, in October I will perform a miracle so that all may believe."

With these words She rose and disappeared into the vastness of space as She had on previous visits. The many phenomenon witnessed by the throng ceased and the reverently quiet people sent up a joyful roar with many thousands of questions to ask the children.

Father João Quaresma turned to Father Manuel Carmo Gois and inquired, "What do you think of that globe, Manuel?" And Father Carmo Gois, who just ten minutes earlier was profoundly negative and quite skeptical, instantly replied, "I think it was the Blessed Virgin," his countenance radiant with enthusiasm.

Above: The three little shepherds in front of the arch that was erected at the site of the apparitions for October 13, 1917

Below: The parents, brothers and sister of Jacinta and Francisco, the father Manuel Pedro Marto (1957) and the mother, Olimpia de Jesus (1956)

"I agree," said João smiling. The two priests began interviewing people and soon realized that not everyone saw the globe or the glowing "snow". Yet many said that they had seen everything but the Virgin Herself. One spectator, the Reverend Doctor Formigão, was not as enthusiastic as these two priests, for he had only seen the decrease in the sun's intensity but nothing else. It was he that would soon be appointed by the bishop to lead the official canonical investigation of these events for the Holy See.

Everyone vowed to return in October. There had been a promise of something special; and special it would be!

The thousands of people who had been coming from far and wide, often great distances, had done so for very good reason. The reports of the very strange happenings and the many cures of sick or crippled people by those who had been eye witnesses were too many to be ignored. By the morning of October 13, 1917, the flow of pilgrims became enormous, and more than 70,000 people filled the Côva in spite of a heavy down-pour of rain.

The Santos family was not happy about the onslaught of humanity that had been pouring across their property. Their beautiful pasture which was their only means of feeding their sheep had been destroyed. The entire area had become a desolate expanse of sand and mud. With no other available means of providing food for their animals, it was necessary to sell the flock before the animals starved. There would be no wool to make thread, then cloth, then clothing for their family. This was a very terrible situation for these simple country folks, leaving them poorer than ever.

Furthermore, there was no longer any privacy with so many hundreds of well-meaning visitors flowing into the Santos and Marto houses at all hours of day and night with their many questions and petitions for the children. Conditions in the little village of Aljustrel had become a nightmare for the two families.

Lùcia's mother, Maria-Rosa, had not yet gone to the Côva to witness any of the phenomena that others were talking about, and simply did not believe any of what she had heard. She thought the entire village and the people from all the towns around had gone mad! She was afraid that there would be serious consequences if the expected "miracle" did not happen; moreover, perhaps her family would be murdered by an angry disappointed crowd.

As days passed, Jacinta and Lùcia were taken to the home of schoolmaster M. Marquês da Cruz in nearby Reixida village to give them a respite from the throngs who had been tormenting them with questions. Soon their retreat was discovered, and many people came there to pursue their questioning.

Maria-Rosa warned the children of the danger, saying, "Dear children, if the miracle you announce does not take place, the crowds will kill you."

To this the children replied, "We are not afraid. The Lady never deceives us. She told us there would be a great miracle and that everyone would be obliged to believe it." Still Maria-Rosa Santos was determined to convince them not to go.

When the morning of October 13th arrived, Lùcia's father, mother and sisters were in a state of great anxiety. Since her mother was in tears, Lùcia comforted her saying, "Dear Mama, nothing will happen to us, Our Lady will do what She has promised to do."

It had continued to rain heavily throughout the morning, so Lùcia took an umbrella and headed for the door. Her mother then jumped to her feet and declared, "If my daughter is going to die, I want to die with her!"

"And so do I," added Tio Antônio. The three under their protective umbrellas proceeded to the Marto house to get the two little ones, pushing their way through the throng in the street.

The Marto house was also filled with visitors sitting on beds and all other furniture. Mother Olímpia Marto was beside herself with all the chaos; yet her husband, Manôel, seemed to enjoy all the commotion. To be heard above the din he shouted gleefully next to her ear, "My dear, don't worry. Now that the house is packed fully, no one else can come in!"

A wealthy and pious woman from the village of Pombalinho had brought two new blue dresses with white veils for the girls as well as garlands of white paper flowers for their heads. The girls looked lovely as they stepped out into the pouring rain beneath umbrellas, but up to their ankles in the muddy street.

Francisco wore his very best Sunday clothes. He looked simply wonderful, notwithstanding his muddy shoes. The walk to the Côva da Iria was difficult with the heavy rain and the many people filling the roadway. At last the entourage arrived at the Côva.

The throng of people was simply enormous. The Catholic newspaper of Lisbon, ORDEM, and the liberal paper, O SECULO, had sent many reporters and both said that the crowd was over 70,000 people. Dr. Almeida Garret of the

Above: A great crowd of over 70,000 gathered in the rain. At noon the great miracle of the sun took place which frightened them, causing many to kneel in the mud and weep. The warm sunshine then dried everyone instantly. Below: The Cove da Iria on October 13, 1917 as the great miracle of the sun took place

Coimbra University who was present felt that there surely was over 100,000 people present.

The people were so densely packed, it was difficult for the three little seers and their families to advance to the rustic arch above the defoliated stump of the small Holm-oak bush. Seeing this problem, a very tall uniformed chauffeur picked up Jacinta and vigorously pushed forward towards the arch with the family in close pursuit. The great crowd pressed in against Tio Marto who was just behind them.

Jacinta, seeing this from her perch, shouted, "Don't crush my father! Don't crush my father!"

Senhora Maria Carreira had arrived earlier, decorated the branchless trunk with many ribbons and flowers, and was standing at the Holm-oak bush in anticipation of the children and the promised miracle. A priest standing nearby asked, "When is the Lady supposed to appear?"

"At noon," replied Lùcia.

The priest looked at his watch saying, "It is already past noon... something seems wrong here." Time passed with no sign of an apparition. Again he removed and looked at his watch saying, "It is past noon," and losing patience and whatever faith he once had, he declared, "This whole affair is an illusion! Let everyone get out of here."

Lùcia, whose faith in the Lady remained inflexible, protested saying, "Whoever wants to go away may do so. But I am not going."

The priest's watch had been on "official" Portuguese government "war time" which was 1.5 hours earlier than natural time. At exactly noon by the sun, Lùcia cried out, "Silence! Be quiet! Our Lady is coming!"

The children fell to their knees; many did likewise closing their umbrellas as the drenching rain had just abruptly stopped. At that moment Senhora Maria-Rosa was enveloped by the sweet floral fragrance she had perceived on Sunday, August 19th when she had taken the branch from Jacinta which she had brought home from Valinhos that day.

The beautiful odor removed the doubt she had borne all these months, and she began to "believe" with tears of joy streaming down her lovely bronzed countenance.

Lùcia had fallen into ecstasy, so Jacinta nudged her saying, "Lùcia, talk to the Lady! She is waiting."

As always before, Lùcia said, "O que é que vossemeçe me quer?" (What do you want of me?")

The Lady replied,

"I want a chapel built here in honor of the Lady of the Rosary. Continue without fail to say the beads every day. The war is going to end, and the soldiers will soon return to their homes."

Knowing that She had promised to say who She is on this day, Lùcia then inquired, "Will you tell me what your name is?"

"I am the Lady of the Rosary," She replied.

Lùcia was delighted by this response and proceeded to recall a list of numerous requests for cures and favors to which Our Lady responded,

"I will grant some of the requests but not all of them. They must amend their lives and ask forgiveness for their sins."

With this Our Lady rose skyward and the miracle of the sun began. Lùcia shouted, "Look at the sun!" The clouds opened revealing the sun as a spinning disk of silver visible without discomfort by everyone. The children alone could see Her in various aspects of Our Lady of Mount Carmel, Lady of Sorrows, Lady of the Rosary, then with Saint Joseph and the Child Jesus, all in their appropriate colored vestments. Our

Lady of Sorrows had no sword piercing Her heart; then came the bust of Our Blessed Savior.

Following these images, the sun began to swirl and cast off beams of colored light in all directions. All of the people looked up without pain at the rotating sun which moved towards earth and back three times, causing thousands to cry for fear of being burned. "Oh my God, we are all going to die! Oh God, forgive us our sins! Mary, save us! I believe, I believe! A miracle, a miracle! This great phenomenon continued for approximately twelve minutes.

Then the sun reversed its zig-zag path, and returned to its normal position with its golden glow of unbearable glare. Many had seen these things in other places as well. Children who were having noon recess and their teachers at Alburitel twelve miles away ran into the street to witness the aerial display. A schoolboy named Inaçio Lourenço Perreira, a lad of nine, stood next to an old man who no longer had practiced religion and had earlier made fun of "the fools" who had gone to Fàtima that day. The boy watched him fall to his knees in the mud, hands heavenward, trembling from head to foot, and crying out, "Nossa Senhora! Nossa Senhora! (Our Lady, Our Lady!)

Two thousand miles to the east it was mid-afternoon in Italy as Rev. Eugenio Pacelli was being consecrated a bishop of the Church. Later, as Pope Pius XII, he admitted to seeing colorful phenomena on the western horizon on his consecration day.

Many cures of grave illness were seen. Maria do Carmo Santos, gravely sick with pain from tuberculosis and a uterine tumor, had made previous difficult trips to Fàtima from her home in Arnal. She had felt better with each visit, but today all her symptoms suddenly disappeared. Those around her marveled at her very instantaneous cure until they realized that they too had been affected in some way by the miracle of the sun.

Everyone who had been soaked from the heavy rain was now completely dry as was the ground beneath their feet. Everyone felt this personal touch of the Virgin Mary and rejoiced exuberantly. There were none who doubted now, for the Queen of Heaven had "moved" heaven and earth to display Her power before the throne of God.

The messages of the Virgin seemed simple, yet they were very complex. Many questions remained and new ones came into being. Why was so much prayer needed? Why would the "Holy Father" suffer greatly? And to which Holy Father did She refer? Perhaps it was not the reigning pope but a future pope yet to be born, for the twentieth century had only just begun.

Thousands await the October 13, 1917 miracle at Fatima

The coat of arms of Pope Saint John Paul II

Pope Saint John Paul II

(1978-2005)

Karol Wojtyla

(May 18, 1920 – April 2, 2005)

CHAPTER 7

The Papal Prophesy Fulfilled

The several thousands of pilgrims who witnessed the great miracle of the sun considered themselves among those privileged to have such an immediate encounter with nonother than the Queen of Heaven. The Côva da Iria became a holy place of pilgrimage where throngs of people from far and near would come to pray. For the rest of the twentieth century, the Côva grew from a pasture to a small village, then a town, and then a city with many buildings which would include hotels for the many visitors, several convents and monasteries of religious orders, and several hospitals for those who come for cures of various ailments.

Within three years of the great miracle, both Francisco and Jacinta had fallen to Influenza and died just as many thousands of others. Yet Lùcia remained strong and healthy throughout the epidemic and beyond, serving God in both Spain and Portugal as a Sister of St. Dorothy and then as a

Carmelite Nun. She was often visited by the Virgin who had promised "never to abandon" her. For as she matured, she realized that she survived with the mission of warning a pope of great danger.

Eventually, Lùcia wrote a letter of warning which was given to her bishop and then transmitted to the Holy See where pope after pope read and pondered the cryptic message. As decades passed, the Church gradually recognized the importance of the visits from heaven; however, it would take many years for the fulfillment of the grave prophesy regarding that, "the Holy Father will have much to suffer."

Throughout the century, many Holy Fathers would endure sufferings and hardships; but to bring the Queen of Heaven personally to give a warning foretold a most devastating and cataclysmic event. For which holy father would She be so concerned? Jewish law allows for vague prophesy understood by few, but forbids detailed "fortune telling" of the future. Which would be the priest so devoted to Her that She would come from heaven to give signs of warning to protect him? Why did She appear on the 13th of May and every 13th again for 6 months? Were these clues that the Virgin was desperately giving? Perhaps this pope had not been born yet in 1917, but may be born shortly thereafter. Let us examine the twentieth century popes to find the answers.

After the death of Pope Leo XIII in 1903, at age 68, Giuseppi Sarto was elected the first pope of the twentieth century taking the name Pius X (1903-1914). He was able to hold on to many conservative doctrinal problems of the day and he performed several miracles of healing in the presence of many witnesses. Yet he was not able to obtain the international peace he sought among European nations; and when World War I broke out in 1914, he died heartbroken within a few days. Very shortly thereafter, he was canonized a saint of the Church.

Pius X was followed by Giacomo della Chiesa who took the name Benedict XV (1914-1922). He was a tireless worker who lead the Church through WW I. He called war "a useless massacre" and would not take sides. He then established normal relations with the Italian state, new diplomatic relations with France and, after three and a half centuries, with England by exchanging representatives. Benedict died of bronchial pneumonia at only 68 years of age.

Then came Pius XI (1922-1939). Achille Ratti was born in Desio, Milan. He renewed the old tradition of blessing Rome and the world from the balcony of St. Peter's Church which had been interrupted when the city of Rome was annexed by the new kingdom of Italy. This gesture was much appreciated by the Italian government and in February 1929 the Lateran Pact Treaty was signed which established the Vatican City State as separate, autonomous, and independent with its own laws, currency, post office and the Pope as sovereign. He was a genius at diplomacy.

The Reverend Eugenio Pacelli (1939-1958) was consecrated a bishop in Rome on October 13, 1917. He later confessed that on the afternoon of his elevation to bishop at the Vatican, he had actually witnessed the miracle of the sun while he was walking in the Vatican garden. He did not mention this until years later. Pacelli was elected pope on March 2, 1939, his 67th birthday, and openly condemned Marxism and Fascism making him a prisoner in the little Vatican state when the forces of Hitler and Mussolini surrounded the area. He took the name Pius XII and though a "prisoner" in the Vatican, he provided great humanitarian service to Jews, opponents of the totalitarian regimes, and finally even the Germans after their defeat. Many Germans were devout Catholics who opposed the evil Nazi party of Adolph Hitler which had taken over their country. Pius was misunderstood by many when he helped those German faithful, suffered great criticism, and he remained a Vatican prisoner until his death. Was he the Holy Father that would have "much to suffer?"

Though he had been gravely ill, when Pius XII, who had reigned for 19 years, died unexpectedly, the College of Cardinals was unprepared to elect a successor. So they elected the seventy-seven-year-old Cardinal Angelo Giuseppe Roncalli, a well-liked, elderly man to be an interim and transitional pope as a compromise between the traditionalist and progressive factions until a "suitable" man could be selected. But Cardinal Roncalli was anything but transitional and took the name John XXIII (1958-1963). This name itself was "controversial" in that an anti-pope had used it centuries earlier in an attempt to "update" the Church at that time! This new Pope John often put on a simple black cassock and wide biretta when he walked alone to his old cobbler friend to have his shoes repaired without any guards.

This caused great concern among the Swiss Guards who were responsible for guarding a pope when he was found "missing" from the papal palace. Later he made regular visits (with guards) to the sick and incarcerated, and stepped down from the papal "pedestal" to show an interest in the problems and sufferings of the people. This pope also welcomed believers, non-believers, and even those who had been excommunicated to papal audiences, thus winning the love and respect of people everywhere. To everyone's great surprise, he called for and opened the Vatican II Council to "bring fresh air" into the church and to consider the many problems of international society as well. He lived to open the Council, but died of a tumor a few months later in 1963. He too, suffered much at his advanced age.

Giovanni Battista Montini then became Pope Paul VI (1963-1978) and completed the work of Vatican II; he served for nearly 15 years making several trips outside the Vatican which included a visit on May 13, 1967 to Fàtima for the 50th anniversary of the apparitions. A statue of him commemorates this first papal visit to the shrine. Pope Paul was followed by Cardinal Albino Luciani, the Patriarch of Venice, who took the name "John-Paul I". He was a modest parish priest who was called "the smiling pope" who held firmly to church teachings, but refused all royal trappings such as being carried on a gestatorial chair or wearing a tiara crown. He died of a heart attack after only 33 days in office although many thought he had been murdered because of his modern abandonment of so many regal customs.

Then came the young bishop Karol Wojtyla of Krakow, Poland who took the name, John-Paul II (1978-2005). He was born on May 18, 1920, just a couple of years after Mary's visit to Fàtima. Karol's family had great devotion to Mary and this devotion carried him through difficult times of his youth in Wadowise where he was born. By the time he was in his teens, he lost his mother, Emilia, of heart and kidney failure on April 13, 1929. Three years later, his older brother Edmund, a medical doctor, died of scarlet fever contracted from a patient in 1932. His father, who had been an army officer, gave him the best education he could on his small lieutenant's salary. Both Karols attended daily Mass at the church across the street from their second-floor apartment. After young Karol completed his own short military requirement with a road construction battalion, the father and son moved to Krakow in 1938 where Karol junior attended Jagiellonian University to study "philology" (linguistics or language study). Young Karol excelled in Latin, Greek, became a literary scholar, and formed the Rhapsodic Theatre drama group with friends.

His father died on August 22, 1941. He served Mass at the Wawel Cathedral for a priest he knew from Wadawice who then lived in Krakow until the Nazis invaded, driving them "underground". It was then that Karol turned to theology and studied for the priesthood in a secret basement room seminary. He was ordained on November 1, 1946; thus he began his journey from priest, to bishop, then cardinal and finally pope.

His audacity as Pope John-Paul II confounded the Communist government when he announced that he would visit his native land in 1979. Those in power could find no excuse to prevent his visit without looking foolish. He came and boldly stated that the division of Europe into East and West, Capitalist and Communist, free and oppressed would not necessarily be permanent. He then met secretly with Lech Walesa, founder of the Solidarity Union, who later became Polish President in 1991. This meeting began the peaceful revolution in Poland which removed Communism from that country and subsequently all of Europe.

As John-Paul's car circled through St. Peter's Square while he blessed the thousands gathered at noon, an attempt was made on his life when three shots were fired at close range on May 13, 1981 by Mehmet Ali Agça. This was exactly 64 years to the hour of Mary's first visit to Fàtima! He would suffer greatly with loss of blood as the car raced to the nearby Gemelli Policlinic where removal of ruined, and the repair of damaged internal organs required five hours of intense surgery. The procedures to save him have been kept secret. Additional surgery was later needed in 1992 to remove an intestinal blockage. The third "secret" given in 1917 to ten-year-old Lùcia and later by her 1940 letter sent to Rome as "the Holy Father would suffer a deathly attack" had indeed happened. Yet by the grace of Mary to Her devoted "son," Karol, he was able to survive, travel to many countries, and lead the Church vigorously until his natural death on April 2, 2005 at the age of 84.

Though he had suffered greatly with several weeks in the hospital and six months of recovery, the Queen of Heaven had intervened and triumphed. A bullet removed from John-Paul's body during surgery has been imbedded into the crown on the statue of the Virgin Mary located within the Basilica at the left side of the main altar at Fàtima.

John-Paul II visited Fàtima, first on May 13, 1982 to thank Mary for protecting him from death by an assassin's bullet, and then again on May 13, 2000 for the solemn beatification of Francisco and Jacinta during which an estimated nearly two million people were present for this outdoor event. A statue of this great pope now graces the plaza at the Fàtima shrine. Many feel that the third and final prophesy has surely been fulfilled.

Since the Basilica of Our Lady completed in 1954 will seat only 2000 people, an immense modern semi-circular, amphitheater style chapel has been built which seats well over 15,000 comfortably and is located at the far end of the area in front of the Basilica. All who visit this wonderful place as a simple pilgrim, leave with a most profound sense of Mary's loving presence and joy. From May to October, many thousands of pilgrims from nations far and wide, come to this beautiful place where many magnificent ceremonies of Eucharistic celebration, music, processions, and devotions enrich the visitors who expect and receive something wonderful. By these marvelous events She continues to draw us to Christ Her Son, "Emmanuel: God with us".

Above: May 13, 1981: Mehmet Ali agca attempts to assassinate Pope John Paul II Below: Crown of Our Lady of Fatima with the bullet embedded

Francisco Marto

CHAPTER 8
Francisco Marto

It would seem strange to people of our time that a perfectly healthy, athletic boy such as Francisco Marto would suddenly become ill and within a few months die. This boy, as well as thousands of other children throughout Europe, were victims of a terribly virulent virus that had not yet been isolated and against which the bodies of Francisco and others were not immune. Vaccines for these types of pestilence were yet to be discovered.

In the early days of the twentieth century, the many advances in the science of medicine, which had begun in the decades following the Civil War, were still under way; and many of these advances were not well known yet in many undeveloped countries. Progress in medical science was a very long and tedious process at best with many scientists delving into unknown areas of nature. There was great resistance to change from centuries old methods of treatments for sickness.

Even washing and cleanliness was slow to become normal medical practice.

Louis Pasteur (December 27, 1822 – September 28, 1895), a French scientist, was convinced that invisible microbes caused many illnesses. He and his wife Marie Laurent had lost three of their five children by typhoid fever. Although his specialty had been the chemistry of crystals, with the loss of three children, he turned all of his efforts to the area of micro-biology.

Thomas Bramwell Welch (December 31, 1825 - December 29, 1903) was born in Glastonbury, England. His father migrated to the United States in 1834 and settled in Watertown, NY. They were Methodists who were against any kind of intoxicating drinks. Welch became a scientist intent on keeping grape juice from fermenting into alcoholic wine. He found that heating the juice for fifteen minutes at only 110 degrees killed the microbes that Pasteur had discovered cause fermentation. Although he became a dentist, his son, Charles (also a dentist) founded the company known today "Welch's Grape Juice Co."

Many other advances in science followed, yet the microbe which caused Influenza had not been isolated. The science of personal hygiene was also in its infancy. Thousands of young people such as Francisco Marto were unable to resist these microbes and fell ill. With their bodies weakened by influenza, other more virulent diseases entered and caused death. The spread of disease became rampant with the movement of troops during the period of World War I. Many young people became severely ill and died when the soldiers that returned from distant wars brought disease home with them.

Francisco Marto was born on June 11, 1908. He was a handsome boy with a round face and small mouth. Though he was only a few months over eight years old in 1917, he was as tall as his ten-year-old cousin, Lucia. He loved music and played tunes on a shepherd's flute. Although of average intelligence, his love of nature moved him to do "experiments" such as feeding sheep's milk to a snake. He also nursed an injured bird back to health. He enjoyed games with his pals, and with his easy-going manner, it did not matter if he won or lost. He also enjoyed playing jokes on his siblings.

He was not much for talking and was usually rather quiet even during games with the other boys. At first, he could not see the vision of Mary; but our Lady told the two girls to have him pray the Rosary. Once he began, "Hail Mary full of grace," the Virgin became fully visible to him. Yet at no time during the six monthly visits could Francisco hear the sound of Mary's voice. It was always necessary for the girls to tell him what She had said.

Once he had seen the vision of Mary, Francisco gradually became extremely quiet and contemplative. He was often found alone in the church with his hand against the tabernacle speaking softly to the hidden Jesus on the other side of the door. No longer did he play games with the other village boys. He had been informed that he would soon go to heaven, so he didn't bother to continue going to school. Instead, he could be found daily in the church with his rosary when not at the Côva tending sheep. Though he was the youngest boy in his family, he was the "man" who protected the sheep and the girls.

One year after the final apparition, in early October of 1918, Francisco fell gravely ill with influenza and was bedridden. He gradually lost weight, probably contracted tuberculosis as well, and became so weak he could hardly pray aloud the rosary with those around his bed. When the parish priest visited him, he asked for Holy Communion. The priest then returned with the Sacrament and Francisco was given his second and last Holy Communion. His first had been from the Angel of Peace.

On the morning of April 4, 1919 with his mother, Olimpia by his bed, a dazzling light came to the door of his room. "Look, mother, do you see that beautiful light there by the door?" he whispered. Our Lady had come for him. Francisco smiled, sighed gently and died at ten o'clock. He was initially buried in a simple grave behind Saint Anthony's Church in Fàtima.

After great difficulty, Francisco's body was found and examined. Only his bones, hair, teeth and rosary remained. These were identified on February 17, 1952 and placed in a small bronze casket. The relics were brought in solemn procession after the construction of the Basilica of Our Lady of the Rosary. These were carried by Francisco's now elderly brothers March 13, 1952 in solemn procession to be reinterred in the side chapel on the right side of the main altar of the then completed Basilica.

On May 13, 2000, Pope John-Paul II beatified both Francisco and his sister Jacinta. Banners depicting each child enlarged to about 75 feet high were hung on either side of the Basilica steeple, which could be easily seen by the million or more people present for the beautiful ceremony which began the process of canonization.

*Banners depicting each child
hung on either side of the Basilica steeple*

Jacinta Marto

CHAPTER 9

Jacinta de Jesus Marto

J acinta Marto was born on March 11, 1910 at the Marto
family house in the small hamlet of Aljustrel which was
part of the village of Fàtima. She was a very tiny and
lovely little girl at age six when she encountered the visions of
the angel and Virgin Mary. Of the nine Marto children, she was
the youngest. Yet her very intelligent father, Manuel Pedro
Marto, knew that she was the most intellectually gifted of his
children and observed her carefully.

Although she was absolutely silent during each vision
that she encountered, Jacinta was usually bubbling over with
talk, remarks and conversation at other times. The presence of
heavenly beings left her awestruck and silent while she ab-
sorbed everything that unfolded in her presence. Her incredible memory recorded everything she encountered.

Although the three children had agreed to tell no one of the magnificent vision of the Virgin Mary they had observed, little Jacinta, after waiting patiently for her two parents to return home, burst into a complete replay of the day's events. While her mother considered it a story of her fertile imagination, her father just listened in silence, knowing that there must surely be some basis for the tale.

Jacinta loved to sing and dance with robust energy. After his first brief visit on September 27, 1917, Father Formigão, the official diocesan inquisitor, wrote of her that, "She is called Jacinta of Jesus, seven years old, pretty tall for her age, slender but not thin, her face well proportioned, dark brown complexion, dressed modestly, her skirt down to her ankles. Her appearance is that of a healthy child, revealing perfect normalcy in her physical and moral aspect."

On the evening of October 13, 1917, when interviewed at home a second time by Father Formigão who had been present earlier that day at the great miracle of the sun, he wrote:

"she was very quiet. The little one did not want
to come to me without her cousin (Lùcia). Very
little, very shy, she finally came to me where I
was sitting. So to appreciate her better, I put
her on a chest and was able to observe her at
will. The pastor had told me she was an angel.
I wanted to see for myself.
I am now convinced she is an "angel" with
much, much love. A large and flowered handkerchief was wrapped around her head. It was
old and ragged. She wore a vest which was not

very clean, and a wide skirt which was the custom of the time. I would like to describe her little face to you; I do not believe I will succeed, but I will at least approximate. The handkerchief, in the way she wore it, made her features even more outstanding, her lovely and charming black eyes, an angelic expression revealing her captivating kindness. Very shy; I had much difficulty hearing the little one's answers to my questions."

Jacinta gradually became at ease with the very gentle, kindly, yet highly educated priest who later made a number of additional interviews with her. The Reverend Manuel Nunes Formigão, Doctor of Canon Law, carefully documented all of the events and happenings of Fàtima as seen by both himself and others.

By the end of 1918, Jacinta contracted Influenza just as her brother had earlier. Her brother had died, so in an attempt to save her, she was taken to the hospital in Vila Nova de Oúrem where she remained for two months during which her mother and Lùcia visited only once because it was a great distance from Fàtima. Since they could do nothing for her there, Jacinta was brought home. Later, when she had developed open sores on her side, Father Formigão persuaded her parents to allow Jacinta to be taken to a large Lisbon hospital because she was losing weight and had become extremely frail.

Though the family had no money for this, a car soon arrived at the Marto house with Father Formigão and Doctor and Mrs. Eurico Lisboa. After a short visit to the Côva and Jacinta's family, the three visitors took Jacinta to Lisbon.

Upon her arrival in Lisbon in January 1920, there was no bed available at the hospital; so Jacinta was brought to a nearby orphanage that was operated by Reverend Mother Maria de Purificaçao Godinho to wait for a bed at the hospital. Mother Godinho personally took care of the little patient and listened carefully to the many things she said. The nun was warm and motherly, a great comfort to a little girl so far away from home. The child was able to visit the convent chapel daily. This was a great comfort to her as well.

Mother Godinho began to record in writing many of the words that the little shepherd said to her, for Jacinta spoke with such authority as if she were not a child, but a grownup. Some of these are listed here:

1) "You must never tell a lie or be lazy, but be very obedient. Do everything well and with patience for love of Our Lord."

2) "Our Lady said that there may be many wars and discords in the world. Wars are only punishments for sins of the world."

3) "If people amend their lives, Our Lord will forgive the world, but if they do not, the punishment will come."

4) "Almighty God will send the world, beginning with Spain, a punishment such as never before has been seen, beginning around the year 1940."

5) "Many marriages are not good; they do not please Our Lord and are not of God."

6) "Pray a great deal for governments. Pity those governments which persecute the religion of Our Lord. If governments left the Church in peace and gave

liberty to the Holy Religion, they would be blessed by God."

7) "My good Mother, do not give yourself to immodest clothes; run away from riches; love holy poverty and silence very much."

8) "Be very charitable even with those who are unkind. Never criticize others, and avoid those who do. Be very patient, for patience brings us to heaven."

9) "Confession is a sacrament of mercy. That is why people should approach the confessional with confidence and joy. Without confession, there is no salvation."

Although it was a long journey and seemed impossible, Mother Godinho told the child that she would love to see the Côva da iria before she died. The child responded, "Don't worry, good Mother, you will go there after my death."

The nun also recorded that Jacinta was visited in her room by Our Lady on several occasions. Once while Reverend Mother was standing at the foot of her bed, Jacinta said, "Move over, dear Mother, because I am expecting Our Lady!"

And sometimes it was a globe of white light, as seen at Fàtima; and the child would say, "This time, it was not like Fàtima, but I knew it was Our Lady."

After each vision of Our Lady, Jacinta would speak with wisdom far beyond her age and the nun would inquire, "who taught you so much?" And her answer would be, "Our Lady taught me, but some things I think out myself. I like to think very much."

On February 2, 1920, Jacinta was finally given a bed at the hospital and Dr. Eurico Lisboa placed her under the care of the leading child care specialists. The diagnosis was purulent pleurisy (severe infection of the left cavity and fistulous osteitis (cracked bones) of the seventh and eighth ribs. These caused the child very excruciating pain. When the doctors prepared her for an operation, she warned them that it would be useless. They removed the two ribs and were hopeful of success even though the wound in her side "was the size of a fist." It was very painful as the nurses cleaned and bathed the wound, yet she never complained.

Mother Godinho visited every day, usually bringing friends. They had happy conversations and four days before her death, she said, "I am not complaining any more. Our Lady has visited again and said She was coming for me soon; and She took all my pains away."

Dr. Lisboa testified that, "Her pains disappeared completely; and she felt inclined to play and busy herself looking at religious pictures, among these was one of Our Lady of the Sameiro. She said that it most resembled Our Lady as she had seen Her." The picture was given to the doctor as a souvenir of Jacinta and was treasured by him.

On February 20, 1920 around 6:00 p.m., Jacinta said she did not feel well and asked for the last rites of the Church. A priest came, heard her confession, and promised to bring her Communion in the morning. She asked for it immediately and insisted that she would die shortly. He felt no reason for alarm, but at 10:30 p.m. she died peacefully with a young nurse, Aurora Gomez whom Jacinta called "Aurorinha," by her side. Nurse Gomez remained with the child's body and in the morning dressed it in a white first Communion dress with blue sash as Jacinta had asked her to do.

Dr. Lisboa knew that in time the Church might accept the apparitions of Fàtima, and did not want her buried in a common grave. He asked a local pastor to allow her body to be placed in a box in the sacristy of his church to await a proper burial. News of Jacinta's death quickly spread throughout Lisbon and crowds flocked to the church to see her and venerate. At first the pastor would not allow this as such homage belonged only to canonized saints; he had the body locked in another room. Crowds still came and just to placate them, the undertaker took small groups to view the little girl.

The undertaker stated that he had never seen such a case as this, and later testified, "It seems to me that I can still today see the little angel. Laid in the casket, she seemed to be still alive in her full beauty, with rosy cheeks and lips. I have seen many bodies in my business, young and old. Never did a thing of this sort happen to me before or since. The pleasant aroma that exhaled from her body cannot be explained. Though the child had been dead three days, the aroma was like a bouquet of flowers."

It should be noted that in Portugal, embalming of bodies is generally not done and burial is usually required and done within 24 hours of death. Jacinta's body had been washed and dressed by the nurse at the hospital; the undertaker had simply placed it in a simple coffin and moved it to the church to await transfer. On February 24 the little body was placed in a leaden casket, sealed in the presence of the authorities and some ladies, and then transferred by train to Ourém to be placed there in the family vault of a generous wealthy man. Mother Godinho accompanied the body; she was thus able to visit Fàtima just as Jacinta had promised.

Tio Marto was at the station to meet the train that brought his little Jacinta home. When he saw the throng of people around the casket being taken from the rail car, he burst into tears like a little child. Fifteen years later, on September

12, 1935, the bishop ordered her body transferred to the Fàtima cemetery for burial in a small tomb with her brother Francisco. Upon examining her casket, her body was found still whole and very much intact.

Upon completion of the large Fàtima Basilica on March 1, 1951, the bodies of both siblings were again transferred to graves in the floor of the left transept. Banners with photos of Jacinta and Francisco, about 75 feet high, were hung on either side of the Basilica's steeple which could be easily seen by the million or so people present for the beautiful ceremony when Pope John-Paul II arrived for the Mass of beatification of the two children on May 13, 2000.

Above: The pilgrims and visitors of Fatima in front of the Shrine of our Lady. Below, left: The flag of Fatima. Below, right: The coat of arms of Fatima

CHAPTER 10

Lucia de Jesus Santos

I t was not by chance that a simple, bright ten-year-old shepherd girl was selected by heaven to take on this very monumental task of delivering the "Fàtima message". Lùcia da Jesus Santos had been visited by an angel to prepare her for what was to come. She was very mature, far beyond her years. This was common knowledge throughout the small village of Aljustrel and beyond. As young as she was at that time, Lùcia was the most sought-after child of all the village as caretaker (e.g. baby-sit) for many families throughout the area. Her way with little ones was most remarkable: playing many games, telling stories and keeping the little ones occupied and well behaved while their parents were busy with many various chores. Indeed, while she was the youngest of her large and busy family, she was totally reliable and dependable. Few girls of only ten years of age exhibit mature qualities such as did Lùcia as the youngest in her large family, and she had them in great abundance. Lùcia's youngest cousins, Francisco and Jacinta, were her constant companions.

They lived only two houses down the street from her in the hamlet of Aljustrel that was a section of the village of Fàtima where their families had lived for generations, and they grew up as part of one big family. Francisco, at age eight, was as tall as Lùcia, and looked after the girls when they were away from the village tending their family's flocks of sheep. Little Jacinta, though not quite six, was very bright and made good conversation with Lùcia who was like a second mother to her. They were a wonderful trio that played, picnicked and tended their sheep together on the land owned by their parents at nearby Loco da Cabeço.

As the grass was consumed by the animals in one area, the little shepherds moved them from area to area with the skill of adult herdsmen. As a result, they knew the area well, and could easily find a cave for shelter during a sudden springtime shower.

The Virgin Mary is often called the "Seat of Wisdom" and indeed She is. Mary sent an angel three times to prepare the children for Her visits. At ages approximately 5, 8, and 10, a visit from the Queen of Heaven would have been quite overwhelming without this preparation. The six monthly visits of Mary during 1917, though only seen by Francisco, also seen and heard by Jacinta, were directed to Lùcia who was the eldest. Lùcia was preserved from the great influenza epidemic which killed many thousands of people during that period, including her two little cousins.

When Mary informed the two siblings that they would go to heaven soon, Lùcia asked, "Will I be left alone?" The Virgin responded that She would never abandon Lùcia, and

She kept Her promise by making several more visits to Lùcia during her life. Throughout her very long life of nearly 98 years, and during her many assignments to convents in Spain as well as Portugal, the Virgin Mary appeared to Lùcia many times; however, Lùcia revealed only a few of these visits.

Since Lùcia was only ten years old in 1917, she did not fully understand all of the things that the Lady from heaven had said to her. These have been called "secrets" (in the then Portuguese language) but might best be called "mystical messages" in modern language. Though the terrible "World War" was just coming to an end, Mary had warned that another even more terrible conflict, "World War II" would follow because so many nations had been turning away from God. This did indeed happen.

The final, "secret" prediction of a murderous assault on "a priest dressed in white" was for many years thought by Lùcia to be the assassination of a pope because priests wore black, bishops wore purple, cardinals wore red and popes wore white. This "secret" had frightened Lùcia severely; and, for a long time, she would not reveal or discuss it. When she became ill at age 36 with pleurisy in June of 1943, for fear that she may die before revealing the "secret," Bishop da Silva wisely "suggested" that she write it down. Yet when she declined to comply, the bishop visited her at the convent in Tuy, Spain on October 1943, and formally ordered her to write down the message. Still she procrastinated until January 2, 1944 when the Virgin Mary appeared to Lùcia to confirm that it was God's will that the message be revealed.

Sister Lùcia struggled with trepidation, and finally on January 9, 1944, Lùcia wrote several lines as best as she could remember on a small piece of paper and sealed it in an envelope but would trust it with no one but Bishop da Silva himself.

The envelope was placed in a notebook and remained there for weeks. Finally, on the 17th of June 1944, Lùcia left Tuy, crossed the Moinho River to Asilio Fonseca where she handed the notebook with the envelope to Archbishop Manuel Maria Ferreira da Silva of Gurza who, the same day, went to deliver it to Bishop Josè Alves da Silva of Leiria at his country home near Braga. Bishop da Silva then took it to his Episcopal palace in Leiria. The message was finally taken to Rome and read by each Pope thereafter.

Pope Pius XII sent the Reverend Joseph Scheigl to interview Lùcia in 1952 regarding the message. Other popes also were aware of the prediction which was written in Portuguese. Pope John XXIII opened Vatican Council II knowing the danger of being out in public. One afternoon he secretly went out to his cobbler for a shoe repair a few blocks from the Vatican palace dressed in a black cassock without telling anyone who he was. Though he enjoyed a pleasant time chatting with his old cobbler friend, this caused a great turmoil while he was missing for several hours. Afterwards, Pope John was always closely guarded by Vatican police who then watched him constantly. There would be no more surprises until elderly Pope John, who was supposed to be what is called "a quiet interim" pope, announced that he would convene the great international Vatican Council II to bring the Church into modern times.

Upon the death of John XXIII, Pope Paul VI worked to complete the Council, and visited the Fàtima Shrine in 1967 to pray for Marian protection, since he wanted to begin several international travels outside the Vatican. His successor, Pope John-Paul I, died just 33 days after his election, and many people thought that he had perhaps been murdered, though there was no kind of evidence for this. He had experienced heart problems for some time, and simply died quietly in his sleep from the stress of the enormous task of the papacy.

Cardinal Karol Wojtyla was then elected pope in 1978 taking the name, John-Paul II. Several years later, when he was shot by Mehmet Ali Agça on May 13, 1981 at very devastatingly close range at exactly sixty-four years to the hour following the Virgin Mary's 1917 visit, there was no doubt that it was this catastrophe that She had predicted. Only the power of the Virgin herself could have prevented the pope's death from such a most incredible attack and by guiding the hands of the physicians during the five-hour surgery at the Gemelli Polyclinic.

After his recovery, Pope John-Paul II made visits to Fàtima and met Sister Lùcia in 1982 during his pilgrimage to thank the Blessed Mother for protecting him. He also traveled there in 1991 and again in 2000 to beatify and begin the canonization process of the two little ones. Sister Lùcia had been transferred to the convent in Coimbra and was able to attend these joyful events with the Pope at Fàtima.

In October of 2004, Lùcia was taken to the hospital for several days of observation for a weakened condition; she reached the age of 97. She was then returned to her convent at Coimbra where she died at 5:25 p.m. on Sunday, February 13, 2005, one month before her 98th birthday with her nephew, Salesian priest, Father Josè dos Santos Valinhos at her bedside. Lùcia Santos had completed her earthly service to the Queen of Heaven.

Pope Saint John Paul II

CHAPTER 11

Priests, Bishops and Pope

Padre Francisco Rodrigues da Cruz
(1859-1948)

Father Francisco da Cruz had been known throughout the land as "The Good Samaritan of Portugal." He was born in Alcochete, Setubal, Portugal in 1859 and was ordained to the priesthood in 1882. His principal duties included the teaching of Philosophy at the Santarem Seminary, directing a school for orphans in Braga, and being spiritual director at the minor seminary in Lisbon. He spent a great deal of his time traveling throughout Portugal visiting prisons and hospitals, giving alms to the poor, and ministering spiritually to everyone. As early as 1880, he wanted to join the Society of Jesus (the Jesuits), but his very busy schedule of service took precedence. In 1929, Pope Pius XI gave the Superior General of the Jesuits permission to accept his vows later on his deathbed; but in 1940, Pope Pius XII allowed him to take vows immediately without making a novitiate or residing in a Jesuit community. He could thus continue his ministry to the poor. He pronounced his vows at the Seminario da Costa in Guimares on December 3, 1940.

He continued his work throughout Portugal (which in those days was still a seriously under developed little country) endearing the multitudes to him. He always carried a small black satchel (cotton bag) filled with alms for the needy. The national government gave him a free pass on all the railroads. Even the Holy Father knew of his work and called him "the saint of Portugal." It was Father Cruz who heard Lùcia dos Santos' first confession at Fàtima in preparation for her first Holy Communion.

His popularity endured for many years after his death in 1948. On April 13, 1951, Cardinal Cerejeira, the Patriarch of Lisbon, opened the ecclesiastical enquiry for the beatification of "Portugal's most famous priest of modern times." In 1959 on the 100th anniversary of his birth, the Portuguese government issued postage stamps with his picture, and in 2009 a postcard with his picture for the 150th anniversary of his birth. A statue of him is located in Revolution Square at Setubal. The cause for his beatification is still being considered.

The Rev. Canon Manuel Nunes Formigão
(1883-1958)

The Rev. Canon Formigão was born on January 1, 1883 at Tomar, Portugal. He was baptized on February 18, 1883 at the church of St. John the Baptist. He was an excellent student, and was sent to Rome in 1903 for advance study. He was ordained a priest on April 4, 1908 in Rome at the age of 25. He was given honors in Theology by the Gregorian University of Rome and the title "Canon" which gives him authority to teach basic and advanced theology.

On his return to Portugal, he visited Lourdes, France and was drawn to deep interest in Marian phenomena. After his return to Portugal in 1917, the Archbishop of Lisbon, Dom Lima Vidal, sent him to do an investigation of the various occurrences being reported in Fàtima which was just a few miles from the seminary in Santarem where he had just begun teaching. Canon Formigão did many very critical interviews with the various visionaries and was sure of their honesty and sincerity. On September 13,1917 he stood only 200 yards from them during the fifth apparition. While he saw only the sun's decrease in intensity and none of the many phenomena seen at that time by many others, he became convinced of the holy visions taking place.

Canon Formigão also witnessed the miracle of the sun on October 13, 1917 together with many thousands of other people. After Francisco and Jacinta died, he arranged with Bishop José Correia da Silva to send Lùcia secretly to be educated by the Dorothean Sisters of Vilar near Oporto in northern Portugal. With Lùcia's identity hidden, she was relieved of the daily questions and interviews of the many visitors which had plagued her.

In addition to his duties as seminary teacher, Canon Formigão also founded "The Blue Army of Our Lady of Fàtima" which now has a large building for its headquarters at the Fàtima complex called "Domus Pacis". He wrote several books and a number of magazine articles of the events which took place at Fàtima. His first book in 1921, "The Marvelous Events of Fàtima" was written under the pen name "The Visconde de Montelo." Often called the fourth seer of Fàtima, Canon Formigão died at the convent in Fàtima on January 30, 1958. He was held in great esteem by the many priests, religious sisters, and students who were privileged to know him.

Dom José Alves Correia da Silva
(1872-1957)

Bishop Jose Alves Correira da Silva was born January 15, 1872 in São Pedro de Fins. He was ordained a priest on August 5, 1894 at only twenty years of age. On July 25, 1920 he was consecrated a bishop by Bishop Antônio Barbosa Leão the Archbishop of Oporto, and he became first bishop of the newly "restored" Diocese of Leiria on August 4, 1920, shortly after the 1917 Fatima apparitions.

The Archbishop of Lisbon had sent Father Formingão (Doctor of Theology and licensed lawyer) from the seminary at Santarem to Fàtima to investigate the happenings there. Bishop da Silva had heard reports of the "alleged" apparitions and the imprisonment of the three children, so Father Formigão was nominated by him to be a member of the diocese's new Canonical Commission to officially study the events at Fàtima. After three trips to Fàtima, interviews with the children, and having witnessed many of the phenomena with others, Formigão reported to Bishop da Silva, "that Fàtima was the place destined by the Queen of Heaven, Patroness of Portugal, for the theatre of Her kindness and mercy."

Bishop da Silva realized that the area around Ajustrel was becoming a place where more and more people considered a "sacred" place to visit. With great wisdom he had the diocese purchase the entire area to avoid exploitation and commercialism. He insisted that people continue to live there just as they had for generations with no changes. Nearby at Fàtima souvenir shops and museums flourish, but at Ajustrel only a few holy monuments and a way of the cross await modern pilgrims to the village. On busy days thousands of people enter the little houses of the seers to observe such things as the little bedroom where Francisco died.

It was not until June 26, 1927 that Bishop da Silva made his first visit to the Côva da Iria where he celebrated Mass that day. Although he had a serious leg ailment, he walked the full ten mile Way of the Cross from Fàtima to the Côva, blessing the fourteen stations and briefly preaching at each one. He did this before firmly believing in the apparitions; however, after the six hour trek from eight a.m to two p.m., Our Lady took this opportunity to repeat for his benefit the mysterious shower of glowing globules that had been seen in both September and October of 1917. This miraculous phenomenon consisted of two elements: a tremendous beam of light coming down from higher regions of the sky, with rays widening as they approached earth, and small shiny white balls falling in the midst of the light. This ended his hesitancy and the bishop then fully believed.

This phenomenon had also been photographed on May 13, 1924 and an authenticated and notarized copy obtained by Senhor Antônio Rebello Matins, the Portuguese vice-consul to the United States, who happened to be at Fàtima. On October 13, 1930, the thirteenth anniversary of the last apparition, in the presence of 100,000 pilgrims, Bishop da Silva declared:

"We deem well to declare worthy of credence the visions of the shepherds at Côva da Iria, in the parish of Fàtima of this diocese, on the 13th day of the months from May to October 1917, and to give official permission for the cult of Our Lady of Fàtima"

José, Bishop of Leiria

At Father Formigão's recommendation, Bishop da Silva sent Lùcia to the Asilo de Vilar school of the Sisters of St. Dorothy in Oporto where on bishop's orders, only Mother Superior was to know her identity. The bishop gave Lùcia strict orders to tell no one else who she was. This freed Lùcia from the daily barrage of many interviewers and allowed her to get a good education. Lùcia loved the Dorothians and joined their order upon her graduation. Bishop da Silva allowed her identity to be known on the day she took her final vows several years later at the convent in Tuy, Spain.

Bishop José Alves da Silva was greatly loved by his people and served as their bishop for thirty-seven years until his holy death on December 4, 1957. He too is buried in the floor of the Basilica of Fàtima.

Pope Saint John-Paul II

Karol Jozef Wojtyla was born on May 18, 1920 in the town of Wadowice, 50 kilometers from the city of Krakow, Poland. He was the youngest of three children born to Karol Wojtyla, a non-commissioned army officer, and his wife Emelia Kaczorowska. A sister, Olga, died before Karol junior was born; and his mother died in 1929. His brother, Edmund, a medical doctor who was somewhat older, died in 1932 of an infection contracted from a patient. Young Karol was baptized on June 20, 1920 by Father Franciszek Zak, received First Holy Communion at age 9, and was confirmed at 18. The two Karols lived together in a second floor apartment just across the street from their parish church where they attended daily Mass. The father died in 1941 leaving young Karol alone.

After graduation from Marcin Wadowita High School, Karol enrolled in Krakow Jagiellonian University's school for drama in 1938. Those studies were interrupted when the Nazi occupational forces closed the University in 1939. Karol was forced to work in a quarry from 1940 to 1944 and then the

Solvay chemical factory to earn his living and avoid being deported to Germany.

By 1942 he became aware of his call to the priesthood and began courses in a clandestine, basement seminary run by Cardinal Adam Stefan Sapiera, the archbishop of Krakow. With long hours of hard labor during the day and many more of intense study at night, young Karol still found time to establish the clandestine "Rhapsodic Theatre" with his thespian friends as a respite from the horror of war. When World War II ended, the major seminary was re-opened and Karol completed his theological studies and was ordained to the priesthood by Cardinal Archbishop Sapiera.

The Cardinal knew Karol well and, being aware of his most unusual intellectual capacity, sent Father Wojtyla to Rome to study under the guidance of the famous French Dominican, Rev. Garrigou-Lagrange, O.P. and in 1948, Karol received a doctorate in theology. He returned to Poland in 1948, and served as vicar to several parishes in Krakow as well as chaplain to university students while also serving as professor of moral theology at the major seminary of Krakow and on the Faculty of Theology of Lubin. His outstanding intellectual gifts were noted by Pope Pius XII who then appointed him auxiliary bishop of Krakow and Archbishop Eugeniusz Baziak consecrated Karol on September 28, 1958 at Wawel Cathedral. Pope Paul VI appointed him archbishop of Krakow on January 13, 1964 and then made him a Cardinal on June 26, 1967.

Bishop Wojtyla participated actively in all the sessions of Vatican Council II and became well known to all the bishops and cardinals of the world. Upon the sudden death of Pope John-Paul I, the cardinals then elected Karol pope on October 16, 1978 at which time he took the name, John-Paul II, making him the 263rd successor to the Apostle. He then served as the most traveled and active pope in history for nearly 27 years.

It was surely John-Paul II who was the "bishop in white" whom the Virgin Mary had warned in 1917 would be assaulted by an assassin. Furthermore, it was Mary who kept Her devoted servant alive during the five-hour surgery to remove the bullets which struck him. In thanksgiving, John-Paul made visits to Fàtima and had one of the bullets embedded in the crown of the statue of Mary located on the left side of the Fàtima Basilica's altar.

The statistics of John-Paul II's works are phenomenal, to list a few:

- 104 pastoral visits outside of Italy attended by millions of people.
- 317 pastoral visits as bishop to Roman parishes.
- 146 pastoral visits within Italy.
- 1160 general audiences on Wednesdays attended by over 17,600,000 pilgrims to Rome.
- 738 audiences with heads of states (kings and presidents).
- 246 audiences with prime ministers (elected or appointed).
- 147 beatification ceremonies proclaiming 1,338 Blessed and 51 Canonizations of saints.
- 231 Cardinals created in 9 consistories (plus one "in pectore".
- 85 important documents: 14 Encyclicals, 15 apostolic Exhortations, 11 Apostolic Constitutions, and 45 Apostolic letters.

- 5 books: "Crossing the Threshold of Hope" (1994)
- "Gift & Mystery on my 50th anniversary of my ordination as Priest" (1996)
- "Roman Triptych" meditations (2003)
- "Arise, Let Us Be Going" (2004)
- "Memory and Identity" (2005)

On Saturday, April 2, 2005 at 9:37 p.m., John-Paul departed this life. Over three million people came to pay homage until his funeral on April 6. On April 28 Pope Benedict XVI waived the waiting period for his canonization; and Cardinal Camillo Ruini, the Vicar General of the Diocese of Rome, officially opened the cause.

On April 27, 2014, Pope Francis declared both Pope John XXIII and Pope John-Paul II to be saints; it was the first double canonization in centuries since Pope Sixtus V founded the process of canonization" in 1588. Thousands had gathered in St. Peter's Square to rejoice at this happy event.

Father Ferreira's Public Letter
Regarding the Fatima Apparitions

F ather Ferreira, the parish priest of St. Anthony's
church in Fatima, was suspected of helping the Administrator of Ourem to kidnap Lucia, Francisco, and
Jacinta on August 13,1917. This was a plausible theory, given
that Father Ferreira was skeptical of and relatively negative towards the events at the Cova da Iria. Moreover, the Administrator, Arturo Santos, had taken the children to Father Ferreira,
and kidnapped them as they left the rectory after talking to the
priest. After a short appearance by Our Lady on August 13, a
large, angry crowd confronted Father Ferreira with their suspi-
cions. In hindsight, it does not appear that Father Ferreira was
involved in the kidnapping. He was merely used as a foil by the
Administrator to seize the children. But tempers remained hot,
and Father Ferreira was threatened numerous times. This
prompted his public letter, in which he sought to exonerate

himself from complicity in the kidnapping. In doing so, he inadvertently affirmed the apparitions, something he had never done, publicly or privately. The letter was published in the Ordem, of Lisbon, and the Ouriense, of Ourem.

TO BELIEVERS AND NON-BELIEVERS:

Reluctantly, as a Catholic priest, I beg to make known and to declare the following before all those who may know or hear rumors — infamous and damaging to my reputation as parish priest — that I was an accomplice in the imprisonment of three children in my parish who assert that they have seen Our Lady. I make this statement on the authority of the parents and for the satisfaction of the 5,000 to 6,000 persons who came many miles and with great sacrifice to see and speak with them. I deny this infamous and insidious calumny, and declare before the whole world that I had nothing whatever to do, directly or indirectly, with this impious and sacrilegious action. The mayor (Arturo Santos, also known as the Administrator, and "the Tinsmith") did not confide his intentions to me. And if it was providential — which it was —that he acted secretly and without any resistance on the part of the children it was no less than providential that the excitement to which this diabolical rumor gave rise was calmed, or the parish would certainly have had to mourn the death of its priest as an accomplice in the crime. That the Devil did not succeed in this, was due certainly to the Virgin Mother. The Mayor, after a protracted interrogation in their own

116

houses, had the children brought to mine under the pretext of collecting more accurate information about the secret which they had refused to reveal to anyone. Then, at the time when he judged it opportune, he ordered them into the carriage, and telling the parents that he was taking them to the Cova da Iria, in fact took them to Vile Nova de Ourem. Why did he choose my house from which to act? In order to escape the consequences of his action? In order that the people should riot, as they did, and accuse me of complicity? Or for some other reason?

I do not know. I only know that I deny all responsibility in the matter, and leave judgment to God. No one can prevent a work of God.

Thousands of eyewitnesses can attest that the presence of the children was not necessary for the Queen of Heaven to manifest Her power. They themselves will attest to the extraordinary phenomena which occurred to confirm their faith. But now, it is not a trio of children, but thousands of people of all ages, classes and conditions who have seen for themselves. If my absence from the Cova, as parish priest, gave offense to believers, my presence as a witness would have been no less objectionable to unbelievers. The Blessed Virgin has no need of the parish priest, in order to manifest Her goodness and the enemies of religion need not tarnish their benevolence by attributing the faith of the people to the presence or otherwise of the parish priest. Faith is a gift of God and not of the priests. This is the true motive of my absence and apparent indifference to such a sublime and marvelous event. This is why I have not replied to the thousand questions and letters, which have been directed to me. The enemy is not asleep, but like a roaring lion. The apostles were not the first to announce the Resurrection. I abstain from any narration of the above-mentioned facts on account of the length of this letter, and because the Press will most certainly have given its own accounts.

I am, your faithfully,

Fr. Manuel Marques Ferreira

Appendix A

The Bishops of
the Diocese of Leiria, Portugal

1545-1556 Brás De Barros CRSA

1556 Fr. Sancho de Moronha e Faro OSA

1556-1579 Gaspar de Casal (Funchal) OESA

1579-1582 António Pinheiro

1583-1604 Pedro de Castilho

1604-1619 Martim Afonso Mexia

1615 Rui Pires da Veiga

1616-1623 António E Santa Maria

*

1625-1627 Francisco de Menezes

F. Robert Roche

1627-1636 Dinis de Mello e Castro

1636-1640 Pedro Barbosa de Eça

1640 Fr. Diogo de Sousa

*

1648 Fr. Jerónimo de Mascarenhas

*

1670-1676 Pedro Viera da Silva

1677-1678 Domingos de Guzmão OP archbishop

1681-1694 José de Lencastre O. Carm.

1694-1746 Álvaro de Abrances e Noroha

1746-1760 João Cosme da Cunha CRSA cardinal

1760-1779 Miguel de Bulhões e Souza OP

1779 Fr. Antônio Bonifácio Coelho

1780-1790 Lourenço de Lencastre

1790-1815 Manuel de Aguiar

1818-1834 João Inácio da Fonseca Manso

1843-1845 Guilherme Henriques de Carvalho cardinal

1846-1851 Manuel José da Costa

1853-1873 Joaquim Pereira Ferraz OSB

1881 The Leiria Diocese Suppressed (to Coimbra)

1918 The Leiria Diocese Restored (from Coimbra)

The Bullet in Mary's Crown

1920-1957 Giuseppe Alves Correia da Silva

1953-1972 João Pereira Venácio

1973-1984 Alberto Cosmé do Amaral

NEW DIOCESE OF LEIRIA-FATIMA ESTABLISHED

1984-1993 Alberto Cosmé do Amaral

1993-2006 Serafim de Sousa Ferreira e Silva

2006- Antônio Augusto dos Santos Marto

* indicates "See" vacant, no bishop

Fr. indicates priest in charge

Appendix B

Visions of the Virgin Mary

Year	Visionary	Location
40	St. James (apostle)	Saragossa, Spain
57	Leo and Simeon	Constantinople
c.250	St. Gregory (Bishop) the Wonderworker	Neo-Caesarea, N. Asia Minor
352	Pope Liberius snow pattern marks	Rome, Italy - spot for St. Mary Major Church
457	Simeon & Emperor Leo	Constantinople
657	St. Ildefonso Bishop of Toledo	Jaen, Andalusia, Spain
708	Bishop Egwin of Worcester	Evesham, England
1061	Richeldis de Faverches	Walsingham, England
1104	Lewes friars move to Thetford Abbey	Thetford, England
1119	St. William Vercelli (d.1142)	Monte Vergine, Italy
1208	St. Domingo de Guzman, OP (c.1170-1221)	Prouille, France
1211	St. Hyacinth, OP (1185-1257)	Odrowaz, Poland

1214	Princess Ermesinde of Luxembourg	Clairefontaine, Luxembourg
c.1220	Bl. Reginald of Orleans, OP	Orleans, France
c.1223	St. Albert the Great, OP	Lauingen, Swabia
c.1225	Margaret of Ypres, TOP	Ypres, France
c.1230	St. Gonsalvo Pereira, OP	Amarante, Portugal
1233	7 men (Servite Order) (August 15, 1233)	Florence, Italy
1251	Friar Simon Stock (July 16, 1251)	Cambridge, England (scapular Mt. Car).
c.1279	Bl. Br. Simon Ballachi, OP	Rimini, Italy
c.1288	St. Agnes Di Segni, OP	Montepulciano, Italy
1294	Holy House of Nazareth (Benedict XIV)	Loreto, Italy
c.1300	Bl. Jordon of Pisa	Pisa, Italy
1326	Gil Cordero (cowherd)	Guadalupe, Spain
c.1325	St. Bridget of Sweden (1303-1373)	Sweden
c.1339	Jon Halldorsson, OP	Bergen, Norway
c.1360	Bl. Villana de Botti, TOP	Florence, Italy
1382	painting by St. Luke (Black Madonna)	Czestochowa, Poland
1397	Bl. Marcolino de Forli, OP	Forli, Italy
1430	Juan Gomez Pedro Sanchez Maria Sanchez Juana Fernandez	Jaen, Andalusia Spain
1467	Petrucci de Geneo (holy painting)	Genazzano, Italy
c.1470	Bl. Alan de la Roche OP (promoter of the Rosary)	Douai, France
1479	Dominica de Paradiso (1st at age 6)	Paradiso, Italy

1481	Bl. Lucy of Narni TOP (1476-1544)	Narni, Italy
1483	Miguel Noguer (November 30, 1483)	El Torn, Spain
1521	St. Inigo Lopez de Loyola	Loyola, Spain
1527	Virgin deters invaders	Frascati, Italy
1531	St. Juan Diego (d.1548, age 57) (Juan Bernardino Diego's uncle, Coatlallope)	Tepeyac, Mexico
1561	St. Teresa of Avila (d.1582, can.1622)	Avila, Spain
c.1585	St. Alphonsus Rodriguez (1531-1617, can.1888)	Majorca, Spain
c.1591	Bl. Peter Martinez, OP	Segovia, Spain
1621	Bl. Peter Bedon, OP	Quito, Peru
c.1623	Bl. Frances Dorothy, OP	Seville, Spain
c.1645	Bl. John Marias, OP	Ribera, Spain
1664	St. Benoite Rencurel (1647-1718)	Le Laus, France
1693	Diego de Vargas	Santa Fe, New Mexico, United States
1700	Giovanni Genovese (BVM painting painted for Guanajuato diocese)	Leon, Mexico
1718	Bl. Benoite Rencurel, OP	Gap, France
1812	Our Lady of Prompt Succor saves New Orleans	New Orleans, Louisiana, United States
1830	St. Catherine Laboure (1806-1876)	Paris, France
1831	St. Seraphim of Sarov (1759-1833)	Sarov, Russia

1842	Alphonse Ratisbonne (1814-1884)	Strasbourg, France
1846	Maximin Giraud (age 11), Melanie Mathieu (age 14)	La Salette, France
1858	St. Bernadette Soubirous (1844-1879)	Massabielle, Lourdes, France
1859	Sr. Adele Brise, OFM-Ter (d. July 5, 1896)	Champion, Wisconsin, United States
1871	Eugene Barbette (12) Joseph Barbette (10) Francoise Richer (11) Jeanne-Marie Lebosse (9) Eugene Freiteau (6)	Pointmain, France
1873	Katharina Hubertus (8) Margaretha Kunz (8) Susanna Leist (8)	Marpingen, Germany
1876	Estelle Faguette	Pellevoisin, France
1876	St. Catherine Laboure (1806-1876)	Paris, France
1879	Revs. Desilets & Frederic	Cap-de-la Madeleine, Quebec, Canada
1879	Rev. Bartholomew Cavanagh Mary McLoughlin Mary Beirne (6) Patrick Hill (13) Bridget French (75) Patrick Walsh (65)	Knock, Ireland
1888	Fabiana Cecchini Serafina G.Valentino	Castelpetroso, Italy
1917	Bl. Francisco Marto (1908-1920) Bl. Jacinta Marto (1910-1921) Bl. Lucia dos Santos	Fatima, Portugal

Year	Name	Location
	(1907-2005)	
1920-1930	Rose Ferron	Woonsocket, Rhode Island, United States
1932-1933	Albert Voisin (age 11) Gilberte Voisin (age 13) Fernande Voisin (age 15) Gilberte Degeimbre (age 9) Andre Degeimbre (age 14)	Beauraing, Belgium
1933	Mariette Beco (age 11)	Banneux, France
1938	St. Faustina Kowalski (1905-1938)	Lodz, Poland
1953	Antonina & Angelo Iannuso	Syracuse, Sicily, Italy
1961-1965	Conchita Gonzales (b. February 7, 1949) Loli Mazon (b. May 1, 1949) Jacinta Cruz (b. April 27, 1949) Maria Cruz (b. June 21, 1950) Maria Dolores Cruz.	Garabandal, Spain
1970+	Veronica Lueken	Bayside, Queens, New York, United States
1968-1971	Cynthia Nelson	Zeitoun, Egypt, Gabal, Dranka (2001), as well as Christians & Moslems
1973	Sister Agnes Katsuko Sasagawa	Akita, Japan
1980	Bernardo Martinez (tailor and parish sexton)	Cuapa, Nicaragua

1980	Thousands witness	Ramses Square, Cairo, Egypt
1981-1989	Agnes Kamagaju (b. 1960) Vestine Salima (b. 1960) Marie-Claire Mukangango (1961-19940) Alphonsine Mumureke (b. 1965) Emanuel Segatashya (1967-1994) Stephanie Mukamurenzi (b. 1968)	Kibeho, Rwanda
1981+	Ivanka Ivankovic (15) Mirjana Dragicevic (16) Jakov Colo (10) Ivan Dragicevic Vicka Ivankovic Marija Pavlovic. (on going visions)	Medjugorje, Bosnia
1986	Rev. Philip Koufos (weeping icon)	Chicago, Illinois, United States
1987	Al. Muharraq Monastery,	Judean, Worcester, Massachusetts, United States
2004	Maria Esperanza of Venezuela (August 7, 2004, age 75)	Ocean City Hospital, New Jersey, United States

c.= approximate date
+ signifies known on going visions as of this writing.

Appendix C

The 20th Century Popes

256   Leo XIII   Vincenzo G. Pecci   1873-1903

Born in Carpineto on March 2, 1810. Upon election blessed the people from within St. Peter's instead of outside in resentment of the then Italian government; first pope to be filmed.

257   St.Pius X   Giuseppe Sarto   1903-1914

Born in Riese Village near Treviso on June 2, 1835. worked many miracles of healing in public. Banned operatic and orchestral music from Mass allowing only pipe organs to support singing in his "Moto Proprio Musicam Ecclesiam".

258   Benedict XV   Giacoma dell Chiesa   1914-1922

Born in Genoa on 21 November 1854 did not take sides during WW-I but worked to make peace helping war victims of both sides. Condemned Modernism as did Pius X. Restored diplomatic relations with Italy, France and with England after four centuries.

259   Pius XI   Achille Ratti   1922-1939

Born in Densi near Milan on 31 May 1857 and as Pope returned the old tradition of blessing Rome and the world from the front balcony of St. Peter's Basilica. He condemned Communism, Fascism and Nazism in memorable encyclicals. Set up Vatican radio; 1st pope to broadcast in Italian.

260   Pius XII   Eugenio Pacelli   1939-1958

Born in Rome March 2, 1876 and was unanimously pope on his birthday March 2, 1939. performed valuable service for war victims including Jews, condemned Marxism, declared dogma of Assumption of Mary.

261   John XXIII   Angelo Giuseppi Roncalli   1958-1963

Born on November 28, 1881 at Sotto il Monto. At nearly age 78 he was elected to be a transition pope, but he convened the Vatican II Council to breathe new life into the church.

262   Paul VI Giovanni Battista Montini   1963-1978

Born on 26 September 1897 in Consesio and kept up the momentum of Pope John's Council and brought it to a close. First 20th century pope to visit many countries.

263   John-Paul I   Albino Lusiani   1978

Born at Canale d'Agordo on 17 October 1912 He died 33 days after his election of a heart attack while asleep.

264   John-Paul II   Karol Wojtyla   1978-2005

Born in Wadowice, Poland on May 18, 1920, first non-Italian pope since Hadrian VI of Holland in 1522. A brilliant scholar, an extensive traveler totally devoted to the Virgin Mary.

Appendix D
Chronology of the Events

Spring 1915 - An angel appears twice to Lucia and three companions: Teresa Matias, Maria Rosa Matias, & Maria Justino; but remains silent.

Spring 1916 - "Angel of Peace" appears as a 15-year-old boy to Lucia and cousins Francisco & Jacinta; is transparent as crystal; teaches them to pray prostrate.

Mid-Summer 1916 - Angel appears to the three again calling himself the "Guardian Angel of Portugal," teaches them the proper way to recite the rosary at the well in Lucia's garden.

Fall 1916 - Angel appears at Cabeco hill near Aljustrel and gives the three children Holy Communion.

May 13, 1917 - 1st apparition of Mary at Cova da Iria ("Cove of St. Irene" [d.653]). (Lucia, Jacinta & Francisco present)

June 13, 1917 - 2nd apparition as in May; rays from Her hands (about 50 people present).

July 13,1917 - 3rd apparition: children shown vision of hell (c. 4,000 people present)

August 13,1917 - children in prison; 4th vision happens on Sunday, August 15 at Valinhos pasture (the 3 children and John Marto are present)

September 13, 1917 - 5th apparition: Virgin promises October miracle, she says don't sleep with rope belts on. (c. 25,000 present)

October 13, 1917 - 6th apparition: Mary asks to have a chapel built; The miracle of the sun takes place with visions of Jesus and several saints. (c. 70,000 to 100,00 present who witness the miracle)

October 23-24 ,1917 - the make-shift shrine is damaged by "pirates".

1918 - little chapel built to replace the shrine.

October 1918 - Francisco contracts Influenza.

April 4, 1919 - Francisco dies at home at 10:00 a.m.; buried in Fatima, St. Anthony's church cemetery.

February 20, 1920 - Jacinta dies in Lisbon hospital at 10:30 p.m.

June 13, 1920 - Statue of Our Lady of Fatima installed at Fatima shrine.

October 12, 1920 - Lucia receives "1st Saturdays" at Ponteverdra.

1921 - Lucia sent to the Dorothian Sisters school at Vilar by Bishop Jose da Silva (Leiria).

March 6,1922 - Capelinha destroyed by dynamite & rebuilt larger.

1926 - Apostolic Nuncio of Lisbon visits Fatima.

1928 - Lucia joins the Dorothian Sisters; first stone is laid for the Sactuario at Fatima.

June 13, 1929 - Virgin Mary appears to Lucia at Tuy, Spain convent requests consecration of Russia to Her Sacred Heart.

September 12, 1935 - Jacinta's body found "intact," moved to Fatima from Vila Nova de Ourem.

1941 - Lucia reveals revelations of wars, atheism, persecution of the church she received in 1917.

October 31, 1942 - Pius XII celebrates the 25th jubilee of his episcopal ordination in Rome which took place the day of the last Fatima apparition. (saw sun miracle from Rome)

1944 - Bishop Da Silva of Leiria receives Part III text.

May 13, 1946 - Pius XII sends Cardinal Masella to Fatima to crown the statue; addresses 800,000 assembled via radio.

1946 - Sr. Lucia visits Fatima to identify various locations of the apparitions.

1948 - Lucia enters the Carmelites, takes the name "Sister Lucia of the Immaculate Heart".

October 13, 1951 - Pope Pius XII sends Cardinal Masella to Fatima to close the Holy Year and reveals that he had seen the "sun" miracle back in 1917.

March 12, 1952 - Francisco's bones found and moved to the Basilica.

May 13, 1956 - Cardinal Roncalli (Patriarch of Venice, later Pope John XXIII) visits Fatima.

May 13, 1967 - Pope Paul VI plans visit to Fatima for 50th anniversary of the apparitions; he invites Lucia to be present.

May 13, 1981 - John-Paul II shot at noon in St. Peter's Square the exact anniversary of the 1st apparition.

May 13, 1982 - John-Paul II visits Fatima says Mass in thanksgiving with Sr. Lucia present (at age 75).

March 25, 1984 - John-Paul II renews world consecration to Mary at Rome.

May 13, 2000 - Cardinal Sodano reveals Part III prophecy and John-Paul II beatifies Francisco and Jacinta.

April 26, 2000 - John Marto (b.1906-d.2000) brother of the seers.

May 16, 2000 - Lucia visits Fatima (home).

February 13, 2005 - Lucia Santos dies at Coimbra convent. (at age 97)

Appendix E
Bibliography

Alonso, Rev.Joaquin Maria CMF, *The Secret of Fàtima*, Cambridge, MA, The Ravengate Press

Fonseca, L. Gonzaga da, *Nossa Senhora de Fàtima*, 1934

Formigão, Rev. Manuel Nunes, *Os Episodias Maravilhosas de Fàtima*, Guarda, Portugal, 1921

Fox, Rev. Robert J., *Rediscovering Fatima*, Huntington, Indiana, Our Sunday Visitor, Inc., 1982 (d. 2009)

Kondor, Rev.Louis, SVD; *Fatima in Lucia's Own Words*, Fàtima, Portugal, Secretariado dos Pastorinhos, (English translation by the Dominican Nuns of Perpetual Rosary, Fàtima), July 2007

Marchi, Rev. John de, IMC, *Fàtima from the Beginning*, Fàtima, Portugal, Edicoes: Missoes Consolata

Marchi, Rev. John de, IMC *The True Story of Fàtima*, Constable, NY, (2009), The Fàtima Center 2009

Marchi. Rev. John de, IMC, *Era Uma Senhora Mais Brilhante Que o Sol*, Fàtima, Portugal, Edicões Missoes Consolata 1946

McGlynn, O.P., Rev. Thomas, *Vision of Fatima*, Boston, Little, Brown & Co, 1948

Pelletier, Joseph A., AA; *The Sun Danced at Fàtima*, Garden City, NY, Image Books, Doubleday & Company, Inc., 1983

Rossi, Rev.Severino and Rev. Aventino de Oliveira (Consolata Fathers), *Fàtima*, Fàtima, Portugal, The Consolata Missions' Publications, translated at the Monastery of Pius XII, 1981

Stanford, Ray; *Fàtima Prophecy*, New York, NY, Ballentine Books, Random House, Inc., 1989

Special thanks to those who gave many suggestions and assisted by proof reading the manuscript including:

JOANNA FRANCES ROCHE ALDEN, A.B. Brown University, French & Education, M.Ed. Bridgewater State college, Latin & Portuguese, University of Maine: Orono: French & Russian.

MARK CHARLES DEAN, A.B. Harvard University, Literature

MICHAEL PHILIP SHAUGHNESSY, B.S. Geo., Salem State University, Travel & Tourism

REV. WILLIAM M. RODRIGUES, A.B. Parochial Vicar, St. Anthony Parish, Taunton. M.Div.

About the Author

F. Robert Roche: was born at home on January 30, 1937 to Francis Roche and Frances (Gonsalves) Roche, and grand-son of Francisco dos Anjos Rocha. To avoid family names confusion, he has used his middle name Robert "Bob" for most of his 81 years.

He arrived one cold January morning, too soon for delivery at Morton Hospital just a block away and was delivered at home at 40 Park Street in Taunton by Dr. Joseph E. Nunes, MD assisted by grandma Maria-Emilia Gonsalves. That was the start of his esoteric journey. Some years later he purchased 62 Park Street where he still lives close to Morton's emergency room!

Following graduation from Taunton High School, he attended Providence College in R.I. where he became a Dominican lay brother and taught Inorganic Chemistry for 6 years after college. While preparing for a teaching career, he worked for the Winters Pipe Organ Co. of Mansfield, MA to pay for his education.

Robert had worked a total of 9 years for Mr. Winters as a school boy; and just before Winters died at 85, he asked "Bob" to take over the work of building and repairing pipe organs for which Bob had been trained. This was a somewhat better job, and for somewhat better pay than teachers were being paid.

The new liturgy of the late 1960's required pipe organs to support singing of both choirs and congregations. Mr. Roche recruited craftsmen from diverse places such as Ireland, France, and several states to assist him as staff of the Roche Pipe Organ Co., Inc. which was located in the old industrial park in the southern part of Taunton.

About forty years ago, a group of organ builders from several states joined him in establishing the American Institute of Organ builders (AIO) to train apprentices in the art. Then a few years later, he was invited to membership in the prestigious International Society of Organ builders (ISO) which meets every other year in a different country. Some wonderful life-long friendships resulted with renowned musicians and many organists from near and far.

Mr. Roche was responsible for 35 new organs of 5 to 60 "stops" from one to three manuals in size, and servicing these and organs by other organ builders from 1960 to 2010. Then the time had come to retire; and now he spends much of his time at his summer home "Villa Rocha" in Portugal and his winters designing organs for churches here in New England and writing texts on several of his favorite technical and religious subjects.

Made in the USA
Middletown, DE
05 November 2019

78017486R00086